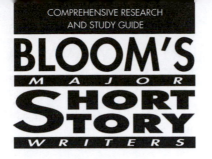

COMPREHENSIVE RESEARCH
AND STUDY GUIDE

BLOOM'S
MAJOR
SHORT
STORY
WRITERS

Thomas
Mann

EDITED AND WITH AN
INTRODUCTION BY HAROLD BLOOM

CURRENTLY AVAILABLE

BLOOM'S MAJOR DRAMATISTS

Aeschylus
Aristophanes
Bertolt Brecht
Anton Chekhov
Henrik Ibsen
Ben Johnson
Christopher
  Marlowe
Arthur Miller
Eugene O'Neill
Shakespeare's
  Comedies
Shakespeare's
  Histories
Shakespeare's
  Romances
Shakespeare's
  Tragedies
George Bernard
  Shaw
Neil Simon
Oscar Wilde
Tennessee
  Williams
August Wilson

BLOOM'S MAJOR NOVELISTS

Jane Austen
The Brontës
Willa Cather
Stephen Crane
Charles Dickens
William Faulkner
F. Scott Fitzgerald
Nathaniel Hawthorne
Ernest Hemingway
Henry James
James Joyce
D. H. Lawrence
Toni Morrison
John Steinbeck
Stendhal
Leo Tolstoy
Mark Twain
Alice Walker
Edith Wharton
Virginia Woolf

BLOOM'S MAJOR POETS

Maya Angelou
Elizabeth Bishop
William Blake
Gwendolyn Brooks
Robert Browning
Geoffrey Chaucer
Sameul Taylor
  Coleridge
Dante
Emily Dickinson
John Donne
H.D.
T. S. Eliot
Robert Frost
Seamus Heaney
Homer
Langston Hughes
John Keats
John Milton
Sylvia Plath
Edgar Allan Poe
Poets of World War I
Shakespeare's Poems
  & Sonnets
Percy Shelley
Alfred, Lord
  Tennyson
Walt Whitman
William Carlos Williams
William Wordsworth
William Butler Yeats

BLOOM'S MAJOR SHORT STORY WRITERS

Jorge Luis Borges
Italo Calvino
Raymond Carver
Anton Chekhov
Joseph Conrad
Stephen Crane
William Faulkner
F. Scott Fitzgerald
Nathaniel Hawthorne
Ernest Hemingway
O. Henry
Shirley Jackson
Henry James
James Joyce
Franz Kafka
D.H. Lawrence
Jack London
Thomas Mann
Herman Melville
Flannery O'Connor
Edgar Allan Poe
Katherine Anne Porter
J. D. Salinger
John Steinbeck
Mark Twain
John Updike
Eudora Welty

COMPREHENSIVE RESEA...
AND STUDY GUIDE...

BLOOM'S
MAJOR
SHORT STORY
WRITERS

Thomas

Mann

EDITED A...   ...D BLOOM

Printed and bound in the United States of America.

First Printing
1 3 5 7 9 8 6 4 2

Library of Congress Cataloging-in-Publication Data

Thomas Mann / Harold Bloom. ed.
     p. cm. — (Bloom's major short story writers)
Includes bibliographical references and index.
     ISBN 0-7910-6819-6
     1. Mann, Thomas, 1875–1955—Criticism and interpretation—Handbooks,
manuals, etc. 2. Mann, Thomas, 1875-1955—Examinations—Study guides.
3. Short story—Examinations—Study guides. 4. Short story—
Handbooks,
manuals, etc. I. Bloom, Harold. II. Series.
   PT2625.A44 Z885 2002
   833'.912—dc21   2002004896

Chelsea House Publishers
1974 Sproul Road, Suite 400
Broomall, PA 19008-0914

The Chelsea House World Wide Web address is http://www.chelseahouse.com

Contributing Editor: Brian Baughan

Layout by EJB Publishing Services

CONTENTS

USER'S GUIDE

This volume is designed to present biographical, critical, and bibliographical information on the author and the author's best-known or most important short stories. Following Harold Bloom's editor's note and introduction is a concise biography of the author that discusses major life events and important literary accomplishments. A plot summary of each story follows, tracing significant themes, patterns, and motifs in the work. An annotated list of characters supplies brief information on the main characters in each story. As with any study guide, it is recommended that the reader read the story beforehand, and have a copy of the story being discussed available for quick reference.

A selection of critical extracts, derived from previously published material, follows each character list. In most cases, these extracts represent the best analysis available from a number of leading critics. Because these extracts are derived from previously published material, they will include the original notations and references when available. Each extract is cited, and readers are encouraged to check the original publication as they continue their research. A bibliography of the author's writings, a list of additional books and articles on the author and their work, and an index of themes and ideas conclude the volume.

ABOUT THE EDITOR

Harold Bloom is Sterling Professor of the Humanities at Yale University and Henry W. and Albert A. Berg Professor of English at the New York University Graduate School. He is the author of over 20 books, and the editor of more than 30 anthologies of literary criticism.

Professor Bloom's works include *Shelly's Mythmaking* (1959), *The Visionary Company* (1961), *Blake's Apocalypse* (1963), *Yeats* (1970), *A Map of Misreading* (1975), *Kabbalah and Criticism* (1975), *Agon: Toward a Theory of Revisionism* (1982), *The American Religion* (1992), *The Western Canon* (1994), and *Omens of Millennium: The Gnosis of Angels, Dreams, and Resurrection* (1996). *The Anxiety of Influence* (1973) sets forth Professor Bloom's provocative theory of the literary relationships between the great writers and their predecessors. His most recent books include *Shakespeare: The Invention of the Human*, a 1998 National Book Award finalist, *How to Read and Why* (2000), and *Stories and Poems for Extremely Intelligent Children of All Ages* (2001).

Professor Bloom earned his Ph.D. from Yale University in 1955 and has served on the Yale faculty since then. He is a 1985 MacArthur Foundation Award recipient and served as the Charles Eliot Norton Professor of Poetry at Harvard University in 1987–88. In 1999 he was awarded the prestigious American Academy of Arts and Letters Gold Medal for Criticism. Professor Bloom is the editor of several other Chelsea House series in literary criticism, including BLOOM'S MAJOR SHORT STORY WRITERS, BLOOM'S MAJOR NOVELISTS, BLOOM'S MAJOR DRAMATISTS, MODERN CRITICAL INTERPRETATIONS, MODERN CRITICAL VIEWS, and BLOOM'S BIOCRITIQUES.

EDITOR'S NOTE

My Introduction, an overview of all five stories, charts the extraordinary variety of Mann's modes of irony.

The classic novella, *Death in Venice*, is one of the perfections of Mann's art. Criticism labors usefully to analyze the intricacies of that perfection. Here William H. McClain examines what appear to be deliberate Wagnerian elements in the story's structure, after which Isadore Traschen finds the hero's journey to be a mythic pattern employed by Mann. Repressed homoerotic desire, fulfillable only in the mind, is traced by J.R. McWilliams, while Ilsedore B. Jonas analyzes the Venetian setting. Shrewdly, Charlotte Rotkin notes the significance of the sea creatures collected by Tadzio, object of Aschenbach's desire, after which Richard White compares the novelist's dream of Dionysiac orgy to the fate of Pentheus in *The Bacchae* of Euripides. Finally, Robert Tobin weaves together the varied emblems of homoeroticism in the novella.

The anti-Fascist allegory, *Mario and the Magician*, is seen is Mann's first major attack in fiction on Hitler, by all seven essayists. Emphases vary: Henry Hatfield centers upon Cipolla's charisma; Allan McIntyre stresses the magician's emptiness; Terri Apter, his aesthetic prominence; Siegfried Mandel, Cipolla's power of transference; Dagmar Barnouw, his Will; Martin Travers returns us to Mann's own politics, while Eva Geulen sees Cipolla's relation to his audience as akin to Mann's effect upon the reader.

The exquisite story, "Disorder and Early Sorrow," is seen as autobiographical by Ignace Feuerlicht, after which Franklin Court reflects upon self-deception as the theme. Sidney Bolkosky features the Professor's longing for the past's glories, while Esther Lesér broods on "order." The sorrows of parenthood are Anthony Heilbut's subject, after which David Turner argues the narrator's assimilation to the Professor.

Tonio Kröger, Mann's portrait of the artist as a boy and as a young man, is studied by Elizabeth Wilkinson as aesthetic alienation, and by Kenneth Wilson as symbolism. The Marxist critic Georg Lukács accurately terms Kröger an eternal bourgeois, while Lida Kirchberger finds the novella's sources in Goethe and in

Theodor Storm. Mann's choice of solitude is stressed by T.J. Reed, after which Beverly Driver Eddy traces Kröger's development.

"Felix Krull," greatly expanded into a late novel by Mann, is considered as self-portrait by Robert B. Heilman and as verbal performance by Erich Heller. The counterpoint manifested in Krull is noted by Matthew Gurewitsch, while Michael Beddow looks at narrative charlatanry, and Martin Swales expounds the theater scene. For Richard Spuler, Krull is Mann as artist of deception, after which Irvin Stock engagingly presents Krull's charm.

Harold Bloom

Thomas Mann's greatest achievements were his novels: *The Magic Mountain, Joseph and his Brothers* (particularly *Tales of Jacob*) and *Doctor Faustus*. But his genius is also manifested in his novellas and stories, which demonstrate—as do the major novels—how he could transform his pervasive irony into a thousand things. Irony in Mann is not so much the condition of literary language itself as it is a composite metaphor for all of his ambivalence towards both self and society.

Death in Venice, no matter how often you reread it, brilliantly refuses to become a period piece. I suspect this is because of Mann's marvelous mask as Aschenbach, who shares both the author's covert homoeroticism and his taste for aesthetic decadence. The irony of Aschenbach's descent into death is that it is simultaneously his awakening to authentic desire.

Mario and the Magician is now perhaps something of a period piece, when Fascism has been replaced by Moslem terror as the enemy. And yet Cipolla lives: he incarnates the dangers of political charisma so permanently that the novella's permanence will return.

"Disorder and Early Sorrow" transcends its socio-economic moment primarily because its vision of a father's love for a little daughter balances irony with an immensely subtle eros.

The novella, *Tonio Kröger*, despite its ironic veneer, does seem to me to have faded. Its bourgeois nostalgias count for less now, and this once, anyway, time's revenges have overcome Mann's ironic stance.

"Felix Krull" however retains all of its ironic exuberance, as does its final expansion into Mann's playful novel of the adventures of Felix Krull, Confidence Man. The too-prevalent image of the artist-as-deceiver is subsumed by Mann's vision of the erotic intensity of the trickster's life.

Thomas Mann

Paul Thomas Mann was born on June 6, 1875, in Lübeck, Germany. His father, Senator Johann Heinrich Mann, was a practical man dedicated to politics and trade. His mother, Julia da Silva-Bruhns, was Brazilian and had an artist's temperament. From an early age Mann was keenly sensitive to his mixed heritage and how it influenced his life and writing.

Throughout childhood and adolescence, Mann was encouraged to write by his mother and his older brother, Heinrich, who also became a famous novelist. His fear that he would have to work for the family's grain firm passed with the premature death of his father. The business, which had been struggling for years, was liquidated soon afterwards. Julia decided to move the family to Munich, where Mann collaborated with his friend Otto Grautoff to publish a literary journal, though it failed after two issues. He then found work as an apprentice clerk at an insurance company, and also enrolled as a part-time student at Munich University.

Mann traveled extensively in his late teens, and when he was 21 he left for Italy to live with Heinrich. There he found inspiration for a number of his works, including his first novel, *Buddenbrooks*. Mann returned two years later to Munich, where his first stories found publication in the weekly periodical *Simplicissimus*. In 1900 he volunteered for the Royal Bavarian Infantry, but within a few months was released due to an inflamed ankle tendon.

The autobiographical *Buddenbrooks*, a tale following four generations of a merchant family, was received as a landmark achievement in German literature. It also introduced several elements found in subsequent works, including Mann's keen psychological insight, his interest in the relationship between art and decadence, and his allegiance to the ideas of Goethe, Schopenhauer, and Nietzsche. The novella *Tonio Kröger* (1903) was also autobiographical, and revealed to Mann's readers his complex appreciation for bourgeois life.

Once he became an established writer, Mann was received in several of Munich's salons. Through one of the salons he met and later married Katja Pringsheim, the daughter of a well-to-do university professor. Several months into their marriage the couple had their first child, Erika Julia Hedwig. They had four more children over the course of the next 14 years, during which time Mann wrote his most famous novella, *Death in Venice*. Mann was familiar with Venice by this point, and found in the city's sultry atmosphere the perfect metaphor for the decadence that corrupts his protagonist, Gustav von Aschenbach.

Mann was an avid supporter of Germany's involvement in World War I. Heinrich, a staunch pacifist, was openly critical of his brother's position. Mann presented a self-defense in a 1918 essay, "Reflections of a Non-Political Man," in which he identified himself exclusively as a poet and a supporter of "culture, soul, freedom and art." However, Mann's apolitical stance was not a permanent one. In his 1922 speech "On the German Republic," he expressed a new political orientation, as well as his disgust with the rising trend of cultural nationalism. The speech was delivered during a lecture tour that Mann took to support his family, who like many German families struggled through a period of postwar inflation. His story "Disorder and Early Sorrow," published in 1925, reflects many national concerns of the time.

The Magic Mountain, published a year before "Disorder and Early Sorrow," marked the apex of Mann's career. When he received the Nobel Prize in 1929—largely for *Buddenbrooks*—he joined the ranks of the great German writers of history. However, the growing power of the Third Reich spelled trouble for Mann and fellow dissenters. Shortly after the publication of *Mario and the Magician*, a political allegory of fascism, he was forced into exile. Mann lived in Switzerland for the next five years, during which Hitler ordered that the author be stripped of his honorary degree from the University of Bonn.

In 1938 Mann left Switzerland to accept a position at Princeton University, where he was a leading anti-Nazi propagandist and an authority on German heritage. In 1941 he moved near his brother, also in exile and living in Pacific Palisades, California. There Mann became a Consultant in Germanic Literature to the Library of Congress. Shortly after becoming an American citizen, Mann published *Doctor Faustus*, one of his most popular novels. At the turn of the decade, the author became distraught over the rising tide of McCarthyism in America, and in 1952 decided to return to Switzerland.

Back in Europe, Mann finished *The Confessions of Felix Krull*, a picaresque novel developed from a fragment written over 40 years earlier. He died of a severe blood clot in 1955, shortly after his 80th birthday. His country soon cleared his reputation as an insurgent, and his accomplishments earned him a place in the canon of German literature. His greatness transcends national boundaries. In the words of his brother Heinrich, Thomas Mann represented "more than himself: a country and its tradition, more, a whole civilization, a supranational consciousness of man in general."

PLOT SUMMARY OF
Death in Venice

Like many of Thomas Mann's short stories and novels, *Death in Venice* presents a blend of myth and psychology, with the familiar scenario of an artist in spiritual crisis. Few of Mann's works, however, sustain a tone as somber as this novella does. Published in 1912, Mann's famous cautionary tale follows a vacationing writer's slow descent into depravity. Readers generally consider the book rich in imagery and classical allusions but simple in concept. In his straightforward description of the novella, Mann called it "a story of death . . . of the voluptuousness of doom."

Gustav von Aschenbach, a solitary writer living in Munich, is re-examining his life in the story's opening pages. Though proud of the self-discipline and hard work that has gained him a great reputation, he approaches the last stages of his career with apprehension. Overwhelmed by the burdens of writing, he fears there is little time left to repeat past achievements. After spending one morning at his desk making little progress, he decides that a walk through the city might clear his mind. As he passes by an old mortuary chapel, a red-haired foreigner standing on the steps captures Aschenbach's eye. The stranger is the first of many anonymous characters who have a mysterious and persuasive effect on Aschenbach. In this case the encounter makes the writer suddenly restless, and he acts on a sudden urge to travel somewhere exotic.

He departs from Munich, and after a brief stay in Pola reveals the Italian port to be not exotic enough, he boards a ship headed south to Venice. During the voyage, he observes with disgust an old, drunken fop trying in vain to pass for a youth. As the boat disembarks, the dandy bids Aschenbach a cryptic farewell, imploring him to "[g]ive her our love, will you, the p-pretty little dear." In the scene immediately following, Aschenbach has an equally puzzling encounter with a gondolier, who without explanation takes a meandering route to Aschenbach's hotel on the Lido. This passage in the novel presents some early signs to the reader that the traveler is headed for danger. Aschenbach enjoys the ride despite the gondolier's odd behavior, and entertains a morbid notion that the cushioned boat in which he sits would make a luxurious coffin. He also experiences feelings of indolence that are totally inconsistent with his ascetic character.

The gondolier finally brings Aschenbach to the Hôtel des Bains. At dinner, later that evening, Aschenbach notices a beautiful, frail Polish boy vacationing with his mother and sisters. Dressed and groomed immaculately, he stands out from his sisters, who are dressed in simple frocks. Aschenbach finds the boy so compelling that he cannot keep his eyes off him. Keeping true to his artistic sensibility, Aschenbach meditates on the formal qualities of the boy's beauty. But his simple longing for the boy is equally strong, and hereafter the story centers on the internal conflict between the rational and sensual parts of Aschenbach's soul. In Nietzschean terms, which many critics often apply to the story, these are the Apollonian and the Dionysian halves of his psyche.

Aschenbach spots the attractive boy again the next day on the beach, and learns after watching him play with his friends that his name is Tadzio. Later in the day, the older man notices the boy's frail qualities, particularly his bluish teeth. He silently observes that Tadzio "will most likely not live to grow old"—a reflection he makes again later in the story.

Meanwhile, the sweltering sea air and the seasonal winds are an increasing source of stress for Aschenbach, who once fell ill under similar weather conditions in Venice as a child. He abruptly decides he must leave, but once aboard the steamer for the train station, he worries that his departure was too hasty. To his surprise, he learns that his bags were sent to the wrong city, giving him an excuse to return to the hotel and wait for his luggage there. He has mixed feelings about the turn of events, realizing that Tadzio is the primary reason why he is happy to be back.

Aschenbach makes no plans to leave Venice again anytime soon, even after his luggage is returned to the hotel. He falls into a routine for a few weeks, arriving early each day to the beach where he knows he can find Tadzio. He picks up his writing again, grateful that he has the boy as a model of perfect beauty, but still disconcerted by the strong emotions swelling up inside of him. He identifies Tadzio with Plato's disciple Phaedrus, who learns from the philosopher the importance of beauty: it is, in Aschenbach's words, "the beauty-lover's way to the spirit." The remaining events of the story decide the truth of Aschenbach's credo.

When Tadzio does not appear at dinner one evening, Aschenbach seeks him out and finds him in front of the hotel. During an exchange of glances, the boy flashes the older man a smile. Aschenbach receives the gesture as a "fatal gift," and when he is alone again he confesses his love, totally aware of the absurdity of his situation.

In the weeks following the incident the writer finds little sleep. He becomes alarmed after smelling a germicide in the air, suspecting the Venetian authorities of hiding an outbreak of cholera. A potential epidemic makes him wonder if Tadzio might leave, and his conscience suffers for fearing the boy's absence. By this point, his interest in Tadzio has become a full-fledged obsession, as he secretively follows him to a church service, and then through canals in a gondola. The germicide is still heavy in the air, and Aschenbach becomes more certain of a large-scale conspiracy. He continues to pursue Tadzio, at one point even stopping in front of the boy's hotel room. With deep regret, he realizes that his dark secret is just as shameful as what he suspects the city is hiding.

There is another peculiar encounter with yet another stranger when a band of street musicians perform at the hotel, with Aschenbach and Tadzio both in attendance. The group is led by a boisterous guitar player, whose physical features are reminiscent of the mysterious gondolier and the stranger in Munich. During the performance the guitarist ventures out into the tables where the hotel guests sit, and Aschenbach snatches the opportunity to quietly confront the musician about the city's secret. The guitarist, unnerved by Aschenbach's questioning, denies everything and rejoins his band to finish the performance, which ends with a raucous number full of whooping laughter. It seems as if the musicians are directly laughing at the hotel guests.

Aschenbach finally receives a straight answer about the epidemic. Cholera has in fact spread throughout the city, already claiming many lives, and Aschenbach is warned to leave as soon as possible. By this point, however, the writer cares little about his own well-being, and is more concerned that Tadzio and his family might leave the city after receiving similar news. He is torn over whether or not he should inform Tadzio's mother about the disease, and eventually decides to remain silent. That night he dreams of a bacchanalian festival, a symbolic outpouring of his many repressed desires. Aschenbach eventually joins the revelers. Though it is only a dream, his final demise is anticipated in this surrender to lust: "In his very soul he tasted the bestial degradation of his fall." The Dionysian element has clearly won the writer over.

More tourists have learned about the epidemic, as Aschenbach notices the Polish family and only a few other hotel guests remain. He visits a barber, who puts makeup on him and dyes his hair, virtually turning Aschenbach into the old fop that he found so repulsive earlier. Aschenbach continues to trail Tadzio wherever he goes, but one day a pursuit through several narrow streets and alleys leaves the man exhausted and weak. As he tries to recover from the ordeal, he renounces all his literary aspirations. In a final ode to Tadzio, whom he once again calls Phaedrus, he concludes that while "beauty is the artist's way to the spirit," the artist is inevitably doomed by a fallen nature that is "prone not to excellence but to excess."

A few days later, an ailing Aschenbach learns that Tadzio and his family are leaving in the afternoon, and so he goes down to the beach to watch the boy one last time. He briefly watches Tadzio wade in the sea, then falls over and dies. The final line of the story reads: "And before nightfall a shocked and respectful world received the news of his decease." His death is inevitable, and thus the reader does not share the same shock as Aschenbach's fans, who have not received this complete account of the writer's fall from grace.

Death in Venice

Gustav von Aschenbach, a self-disciplined and successful writer living in Munich, has recently felt frustrated with his work. An uncharacteristic craving for travel brings him to Venice, where the beauty of a Polish boy inspires him to write again. The boy's beauty also sparks an irrepressible passion in the artist that ultimately leads to his ruin.

Tadzio is a 14-year-old Polish boy vacationing in the same hotel in Venice as Aschenbach. A blond naïf with godlike beauty, he is the object of Aschenbach's burgeoning obsession.

The stranger in Munich, a red-headed foreigner wearing a straw hat, catches Aschenbach's gaze when he finds him on the steps of a mortuary chapel. Though the two never exchange words, something in the man's exotic appearance makes Aschenbach suddenly restless.

The sinister gondolier is another mysterious stranger whom Aschenbach encounters during his travels. While transporting Aschenbach to his hotel, he ignores his instructions, and after arriving Aschenbach learns that he is not a licensed gondolier.

The old dandy, an obnoxiously loud drunk accompanying a group of lively young men, travels aboard the same ship that Aschenbach takes to Venice. Wearing false teeth and a wig, he perplexes the writer, who doesn't understand why the youths accept him as one of their own.

The street musician is the charismatic guitarist and leader of a Venetian band who performs at Aschenbach's hotel. He wins the crowd over with his stage antics, and only once loses his boldness, when Aschenbach confronts him about the cholera outbreak.

Death in Venice

WILLIAM H. MCCLAIN ON WAGNER'S INFLUENCE

[The late William H. McClain taught in the German department at Johns Hopkins University and wrote *Between Real
and Ideal*, an analysis of the works of German novelist Otto
Ludwig. Here he discusses structural similarities between
the novella and Richard Wagner's music-dramas.]

Far more important than the resemblances between Mann's hero and
Wagner, of course, are the deeper-lying similarities in form and content between Mann's *Novelle* and Wagner's music-dramas. One of
the most basic of these is that *Der Tod in Venedig* was also consciously composed as a mythological work. Mann often spoke
admiringly of Wagner's ability to create myths and in his lecture on
Der Ring des Nibelungen in the Aula of the University of Zürich in
November 1937 even went so far as to suggest that through his
mythological figures Wagner succeeded in expressing something
akin to what Jung called the collective unconscious. His remarks
about his own art indicate that he also thought of himself as a mythological writer. In *Freud und die Zukunft* he characterizes this type of
writer (clearly referring to himself) as one who has acquired the
habit of regarding all of life and reality as mythical and hence typical. When a writer has learned to look at reality in this way, he continues, he experiences a heightening of his perceptive powers which
enables him to see how the lives of all human beings, even of prominent individuals, are in a larger sense merely formula and repetition.
(. . .)

If the overtones of *Der Tod in Venedig* cause it to seem musically
composed, its thematic structure even tempts one to feel that Mann
may consciously have composed it in Wagnerian style; for his inter-
weaving of themes and motives is strikingly reminiscent of the "the-
matisch-motivische Gewebstechnik" which he cites as Wagner's
great innovation in his lecture on *Der Ring des Nibelungen*. Those
who think of Wagner as a composer and as a man of the theater may

be astonished to discover that Mann tended to regard him as an epic writer and even considered the *Leitmotiv* as an epic device. It was moreover Wagner's epic qualities which attracted him most, he confesses in his *Auseinandersetzung mit Richard Wagner* in 1908, and freely admits that it is not difficult "in meinen 'Buddenbrooks,' diesem epischen, von Leitmotiven verknüpften und durchwobenen Generationenzuge, vom Geiste des 'Nibelungenringes' einen Hauch zu verspüren." We feel this spirit even more strongly in *Der Tod in Venedig*. If we analyze the thematic structure of the *Novelle* as we would the score of a Wagnerian music-drama, we discover that it, too, is built on *Leitmotive*; that seven stand out as the main ones; and that as the *Novelle* progresses each, like Wagner's, undergoes subtle metamorphoses and acquires different shades of meaning or tone-feeling. We also note that Mann combines his *Leitmotive* as Wagner does. If, following the practice of Ernest Newman, we label the *Leitmotive* for convenience in referring to them, we might say that the first we hear is the motive of falseness, which is sounded at the very beginning of the story in the passage describing the false mid-summer weather. It is repeated, in different orchestration, as it were, in the figure of the old man wearing the mask of youth on the ship which takes Aschenbach to Venice; in the sequence describing Aschenbach's ride in the illegally operated gondola; in his conscious concealment of the cholera epidemic; and in his donning of the mask of youth in the barber shop. The second great *Leitmotiv*, also introduced at the beginning, could be called the motive of encounter. It is first heard in the passage describing the confrontation with the provocative figure in the mortuary door, recurs in modulated form in the meeting with Tadzio, and sings out once more gloriously in the final scene which brings the encounter with death. The third *Leitmotiv*, also sounded at the beginning, might be labeled the motive of yearning. It first occurs in the form of Aschenbach's longing to slough off the heavy burden of creative work and recurs later both in his passionate longing for beauty, as he discovers it in incarnate form in Tadzio, and in the unconscious longing for the final freedom and repose of death which develops by almost imperceptible stages out of his initial "Begierde nach Befreiung, Entbürdung und Vergessen" as the tale progresses. A fourth *Leitmotiv*, likewise introduced at an early point, is the death-motive, which we first hear in the sequence depicting the figure in the mortuary door and later, in metamorphosed form, in the passage describing Aschenbach's strange gondola ride after his arrival in Venice; in the scene where the strolling singers perform in the hotel garden; and in the final scene. This *Leitmotiv* is combined early in the story with a fifth, which we might call the motive of fleeting-time; and later it also combines with two others, the love-motive, or Eros-motive, and what we might call the nirvana-motive, or the motive of the absolute. The element which enables Aschenbach to approximate the experience of the absolute, we are told, is the sea; and the motive of the absolute accordingly first occurs in the passage describing the artist's profound love of the sea. We hear it subsequently in every passage describing the sea.

—William H. McClain, "Wagnerian Overtones in 'Der Tod in Venedig.'" *Modern Language Notes* 79 (1964): pp. 487–88, 489–91.

ISADORE TRASCHEN ON THE MYTHIC PATTERN

[Isadore Traschen taught in the Humanities department at Rensselaer Polytechnic Institute in Troy, New York, and co-edited (with James R. Frakes) *Short Fiction: A Critical Collection*. In addition to criticism on Thomas Mann, he also published essays on Henry James, Fyodor Dostoevsky, and Robert Frost. In this extract, he explains how the hero's mythic journey gives shape to Mann's narrative.]

IN REVIEWING Joyce's *Ulysses* in 1923 T. S. Eliot observed that "In using the myth [of the *Odyssey*], in manipulating a continuous parallel between contemporaneity and antiquity, Mr. Joyce is pursuing a method which others must pursue after him. . . . It is simply a way of controlling, of ordering, of giving shape and a significance to the immense panorama of futility and anarchy which is contemporary history. It is a method already adumbrated by Mr. Yeats, and of the need for which I believe Mr. Yeats to have been the first contemporary to be conscious. . . . Instead of the narrative method, we may now use the mythical method." Eliot was, of course, affirming his own practice as well, his re-creation the year before of the "long narrative poem" in *The Wasteland*. Yet, as we know, back in 1911

Thomas Mann had already employed the mythical method in giving shape to "Death in Venice" by drawing upon Nietzsche's concept of the Apollonian-Dionysian mythology in *The Birth of Tragedy*. But Mann anticipated Joyce and Eliot by drawing upon still another area of myth, one apparently disguised so well that it has gone unnoticed. This area of myth has been established by Joseph Campbell in his exhaustive and brilliant study, *The Hero with a Thousand Faces*. This study reveals that the heroes of mythology undergo a common pattern of experience; Campbell calls this pattern the monomyth. The monomythic pattern is that of the Adventure of the Hero, divided into the phases of Departure, Initiation, and Return. Gustave von Aschenbach, Mann's hero, does not return. Thus the last phase of the monomyth points to the difference between the divine comedy—the reunion with the Deity—which actually or figuratively shapes the old myths, and the tragedy which shapes "Death in Venice." The mythic hero's adventure takes place in a world which, even if haunted by unfriendly spirits, is nonetheless made for him; Aschenbach's adventure takes place in a world he does not belong to, a formless, polyglot, perverse, cosmopolitan society. This difference in the last phase suggests that Mann will use the mythic pattern ironically, parodistically, again anticipating Joyce and Eliot.

"Death in Venice," then, embodies two primary myths, the Apollonian-Dionysian and the monomyth. But what I have said about the corresponding patterns of Mann's tale and the monomyth is hardly sufficient evidence that Mann was drawing upon this mythic type; *bildungsroman* and picaresque novels can be shown to have the same pattern, with a "happy" ending. That Mann would have turned to myth is likely from his own earlier work, stimulated as it was by the strong disposition toward myth in the nineteenth century, particularly in Germany.

—Isadore Traschen, "The Uses of Myth in 'Death in Venice.'" *Modern Fiction Studies* 11, no. 2 (Summer 1965): pp. 165–66.

J. R. McWilliams on Repression

[J. R. McWilliams is Associate Professor Emeritus of German at University of Oregon and author of *Brother*

Artist: A Psychological Study of Thomas Mann's Fiction. In this excerpt he discusses the ways in which Aschenbach seeks gratification for his repressed desires.]

Here there is still an element of the Tonio Kröger repression in the artist who numbs and attenuates his passions by the intellectual process of creation. But after Tadzio has once responded by a smile to the voyeuristic sallies of the hero, the latter's striving for beauty assumes the features of the perverse culminating in the orgiastic dream. (. . .)

The u-sound, a reference to the Polish pronunciation of the beautiful boy's name, Tadzio, is the lure to the depths of Aschenbach's fall and degradation. In his Bacchanalian vision he achieves instinctual gratification, in essence the revenge of his capped impulses. It is readily seen that love, normally associated with tenderness, is utterly lacking in this scene. The hero's ability to love had long since been severely crippled. What we find in his dream consummation of sex is sensual gratification with unmistakable elements of cruelty, aggression and destruction. This dream offers convincing evidence of Aschenbach's ambivalence; in his mind the sexual is never dissociated from death. As horribly degrading as his dream is, it is still the logical consequence of the harsh stringency he has imposed on his drives. Degradation means for him a measure of punishment and, as such, atonement. It also weakens his carefully constructed prohibitions against unrestrained behaviour. Further, the frenzy of the debauch points to the pleasures in store for him, if he will let himself go. This is why the dream shatters him; it represents an irresistible step towards ruin, helps to pave the way for his death through the plague, and at the same time gives further sanctions to his burning transgressions.

After the dream orgy Aschenbach wears foppish clothes and lets himself be painted with cosmetics, in order to become attractive to Tadzio. He now contrasts strikingly with the impeccably dressed Tonio Kröger who abhors the Bohemian type and all his lax ways. Aschenbach's willingness to experience abasement shows us that he is close to death. For in his self-imposed humiliation he is intentionally seeking out that which he fears in order to steel himself against too sudden exposure. He hopes thereby to prove that he is the arbiter of his own destiny and not totally subject to unknown forces. By arranging the humiliation himself he dispels his fear of the consequences.

The actual cause of Aschenbach's death is treated so casually that the reader is apt to miss the terse statements which describe his eating of the overripe strawberries. Matter of factly and desultorily Aschenbach partakes of them on a stroll through the city. The offhand and brief manner of this presentation contrasts sharply with the minute history of his adventures in Venice. Yet this description too fits the psychological needs of the hero. Though consciously aware of the dangers of the pestilence, his haphazard and unthinking feast of the moment allays his fear of falling directly a victim to the plague. He does not reflectively dwell on the possible consequences of his act, but rather inadvertently stills his momentary and insignificant need for refreshment. In this way he prevents the knowledge of his own fate from being consciously apprehended by rational thought.

Only after he has exposed himself to the perils of disease can gratification occur. As in the case with Albrecht van der Qualen in *Der Kleiderschrank*, a decree of death is a contingency of the penalty for instinctual release. Only then are the ends of retributive justice satisfied. In the final scene Tadzio is overcome in a wrestling bout by his black-haired companion Jaschiu. Through this substitute symbolic contact is made between the lover and the beloved. Moments later Aschenbach dies. Consummation has exacted the final payment.

Nowhere else in his works has Thomas Mann given us such a look at the ghastly and shocking results of unrestricted indulgence. Yet, paradoxically, Gustav Aschenbach's passion for Tadzio is completely passive. Everything is at a distance. From afar he gazes longingly at the object of his love. Once he walks behind Tadzio and is overcome by the desire to touch him, but at the last moment he hesitates and successfully resists the urge. This is the closest he comes to putting his amorous designs into action. It is true that he destroys his *dehors* by letting himself be painted with cosmetics and that he shadows Tadzio through the streets of the city, but his love affair never progresses beyond the point of voyeurism. Consummation is all in his mind.

—J. R. McWilliams, "The Failure of a Repression: Thomas Mann's 'Tod in Venedig.'" *German Life & Letters* 20 (1966–67): pp. 238–40.

ILSEDORE B. JONAS ON THE SETTING

[Ilsedore B. Jonas has published works on Rainer Maria Rilke and Thomas Mann, and with Klaus W. Jonas compiled a bibliography of Mann criticism. In the following excerpt taken from her book *Thomas Mann and Italy*, she discusses the effect of the exotic setting on Aschenbach.]

In the novella *Death in Venice* (*Der Tod in Venedig*) Mann assigned to the city of lagoons—which (as was discussed in our first chapter) was very dear to his heart and which, on his visits, had again and again deeply impressed him anew—a rôle important, actually crucial, to the development of the action. In the drama *Fiorenza* of 1905, the Italian landscape is still of very minor importance: in the second act the writer leads us into the garden of the Villa Medici, where "the open Campagna with cypresses, stone-pines and olive trees" extended into the distance. The Florence of the Renaissance is only a backdrop in front of which the problematics of the characters are brought into relief. In the novella *Death in Venice*, on the other hand, the city of Venice and the landscape surrounding it—that is, in this case, the sea—are of determining significance; indeed, actually a part of the action itself.

Romantic Venice, the Venice of Platen, Wagner, and Nietzsche, reflects an older cultural epoch and is yet at the same time a city of the modern. And Thomas Mann, the stylistic artist, succeeds, through the help of the description of the real world, in fashioning a rich symbolism.

Before Aschenbach, the hero of the novella, decides upon his trip to Italy, he has, in Munich, the vision of a wild, exotic landscape: "a tropical swampland under a thick, steamy sky, humid, rank and monstrous, a kind of primeval jungle wilderness of islands, morasses and slime-bearing channels." He decides to prepare for the trip, for a puzzling yearning has seized him, a longing for such a landscape which will enable him, after all his self-imposed discipline and narrow existence, to let all restraint fall away and to find his true self.

For Aschenbach there is no doubt that the south will bring him the fulfillment of his wish for self-release. Just as the heroes of Thomas Mann's early novellas—Paolo Hofmann, the Dilettante and Tonio

Kröger—Aschenbach also travels to Italy, since by means of its colorful, spirited animation he promises himself deliverance from his previous isolation and self-discipline. Thus he comes to Venice, and on seeing this city recollections come alive in him of the poet Platen, that "melancholy and enthusiastic" poet, "for whom once upon a time the domes and bell-towers of his dreams had risen from these waters."

With every fibre Aschenbach drinks in the fabulous beauty of Venice as he glides slowly on the ship through the canal of San Marco, and he is delighted that by the open sea he reaches this city, whose character is so strongly defined by the water surrounding and penetrating it:

> Then he saw it again, the most remarkable landing place, that dazzling composition of fantastic structures which the Republic set facing the awestruck gaze of approaching seafarers: the graceful magnificence of the palace and the Bridge of Sighs, the columns with lion and saint by the shore, the splendid projecting flank of the fairy-tale temple, the vista of archway and clock of the giants, and looking at it he reflected that arriving in Venice by land at the railway station is the same as entering a palace through a back door, and that in no other way except as he was now, except across the high seas, should one arrive at the most improbable of cities.

Yet the impression of beauty and incredibility becomes supplanted by a feeling of dread as Gustav von Aschenbach enters the gondola which is to bring him out to the Lido. Suddenly he becomes distinctly conscious of how much in form and color it (the gondola) resembles a coffin: "Who might not have to subdue a fleeting terror, a secret aversion and uneasiness, when for the first time or after a long absence the moment came to step into a Venetian gondola? That peculiar craft, handed down completely unchanged from balladesque times and so singularly black, as otherwise only coffins are among all things,—it calls to mind silent and criminal adventures in the plashing night, still more it calls to mind death itself, the bier and mournful funeral and last, silent voyage."

The sweet, exotic fullness of life which seduces the visitor from the north into erotic adventures now becomes intimately fused with the motif of extreme danger, indeed, of inescapable destruction. But simultaneously, in this work Italy, for the first time for Thomas

Mann, also signifies the land of antiquity. He described the figure of the boy Tadzio with all the attributes of a noble Greek sculpture, of the kind he had studied closely in the museums on his first visit to Italy. "The head of Eros, out of the yellowish mellowness of Parian marble, with fine and serious brows, temples and ears duskily and softly hidden by the springing ringlets of his hair."

The danger to Aschenbach from the ominous atmosphere of the city, hidden beneath the magnificence and "splendor," emerges in the ever more strongly emphasized picture of decay and putrefaction: "A loathesome sultriness lay in the narrow streets; the air was so heavy that the smells which issued from dwellings, shops, eating-houses, oil fumes, clouds of perfume and many others lay in exhalations, without dissipating." Aschenbach begins to feel unwell, until finally he knows that he must leave. "The longer he walked, the more agonizingly he was seized by the abominable state which the sea air combined with the sirocco can produce, and which is at the same time stimulating and enervating." He has himself conveyed to San Marco by gondola. Yet on the trip the fascination of Venice, which has become ambiguous for him, wraps Aschenbach in its spell: "through the gloomy labyrinth of the canals, beneath delicate marble balconies, past grieving palace façades."

—Ilsedore B. Jonas, *Thomas Mann and Italy*, trans. Betty Crouse (Tuscaloosa: University of Alabama Press, 1979): pp. 34–36.

CHARLOTTE ROTKIN ON THE SEA CREATURES

[Charlotte Rotkin, a former Assistant Professor of English at Pace University in New York City, retired in 1972. Along with her collections of poems, she has also published a critical analysis, *Deception in Dickens' Little Dorritt*. Here she discusses the overlooked significance of the sea creatures collected by Tadzio.]

Critical commentary has focused on the archetypal symbolism of the sea in terms of its prototypical pattern of death and rebirth. However, scant attention has been accorded the allegorical significance of sea shells, sea horses, jellyfish, and sidewards-running crabs. The disclosure of the interrelationship of seemingly superficial sea animals reinforces Mann's criticism of moral lassitude, which he equates with a denial of life and art. His ironic enumeration of the sea creatures both parallels and illustrates the importance of their function to characterization and conclusion. The connotative meaning of each oceanic organism reverberates backward and forward to presage Aschenbach's behavior and to make manifest the pattern of his prior actions in the conflict between volition and eros.

Engaged in an inner conflict between the contradictory forces of discipline and lust, Aschenbach increasingly succumbs to the lyricism inherent in the Dionysiac. When Tadzio emerges from the ocean to show his mother the sea animals he has found, Aschenbach does not understand one word the Polish youth utters, but to him Tadzio's unintelligible sounds become "mingled harmonies" (43). On an allegorical level, the unleashing of the Dionysiac functions as a foreign and fascinating tongue to Aschenbach.

The merged harmonies of the exotic language serve several purposes for Mann in defining the relationships between Tadzio, his mother, and Aschenbach. On one plane the mother's presence thwarts any possibility of commingling between Tadzio and Aschenbach. On another level the mother's close proximity to her son reinforces the image of the existing harmony between them. The mother hovers in the background, a regal figure in grey, adorned with fabulous pearls, "the size of cherries" (27). The image Mann creates for her is emblematic; the objectified symbol consists of the pearls which the reader envisions whenever reference is made to her. In addition, her portrait reveals an unspecified concept. The mother has produced a fabulous creature and dressed him in decorative attire, as the sea has spawned the astonishing pearls the mother wears to adorn her garments. The exceptional beauty of her pearls and of her son signify the mother's possessions, and, reverberating, connote the archetypal maternal symbolism of sea, pearl, and power.

The segment of the tale in which Tadzio captures the sea treasures, operates on multifarious strata to strengthen characterization and to foreshadow conclusion by its sequential ordering of imagery. The symbolic significance of sea shells, sea horses, jellyfish, and sidewards-running crabs echoes backward and forward to recall Aschenbach's previous behavior and to prefigure his future indecisiveness. Structurally, the scene interweaves the ironic discussion of moral resolution at the beginning of the narrative with the similarly ironic address to Phaedrus at the end. Strategically situated at mid-point in the novella, this allegorical scene illustrates Aschenbach's failure of moral resolve and foretells his tragic death. The shells, sea horses, jellyfish, and side-stepping crabs strengthen the thematic fabric of the tale by evoking four corresponding symbols of pearls, sensuality, weakness, and evasion. The shells, jellyfish, and crabs suggest generally accepted connotations, in contrast to that of the sea horse. The interpretation of the symbolism of the sea horse bears a resemblance to the process of dream analysis that Freud describes. Freud states that the analysand's personal associations are essential to the analyst's interpretation of the patient's dream. The sea horse, summoning forth sensuality, is a poetic symbol deriving solely from the complex of associations that Mann has created within the novella.

The represented images of the sea creatures, operating on alle-gorical and philosophical planes, intertwine the figures of mother, Tadzio, and Aschenbach. Each specified form of sea life connotes a multiplicity of meanings in direct proportion to the order in which it is enumerated in the series. Shells suggest images of the hard outer covering of mullusks, which conjure images of pearls, which evoke a picture of the mother. Sea horses inspire images of prehensile tails, which connote the notion of seizing, which summons the idea of the sensuality that has taken possession of Aschenbach via Tadzio, who has captured the sea horse. Jellyfish elicit increasingly vivid images: the vision of trailing tentacles which reinforces the concept of pre-hensility, in addition to the image of Medusa, which prompts an image of Tadzio's alluringly disheveled hair. In the vernacular, the idea called forth by jellyfish is one of human weakness. Retrospectively, the latter idea contains an ironic reference to Aschenbach, an allusion whose total implication remains elusive until the conclusion of the novella. Sidewards-running crabs under-score the moral choice Aschenbach neglects to make at the end of the story. The side-stepping crabs invoke the mental image of the cir-cuitous route by which Aschenbach's feelings of lethargy led him "to go a journey" (8).

—Charlotte Rotkin, "Oceanic Animals: Allegory in 'Death in Venice.'" *Papers on Language & Literature* 23, no. 1 (Winter 1987): pp. 84, 85–87.

RICHARD WHITE ON THE PROTAGONIST'S DREAM

[Richard White is Associate Professor of Philosophy at Creighton University in Omaha, Nebraska, and is author of *Nietzsche and the Problem of Sovereignty*. In this excerpt he draws a comparison between Aschenbach's dream and Euripides' play *The Bacchae*.]

After establishing Aschenbach's severe self-mastery at the beginning, the rest of *Death in Venice* records the gradual undermining of his resolve. Thus, almost as soon as he arrives in Venice, Aschenbach begins to experience the pull of an alien force which gradually overcomes his will and destroys his self-mastery; and he quickly abandons himself to his obsession for Tadzio. When the mysterious gondolier rows him to the Lido against his wishes, the normally self-possessed Aschenbach finds it impossible to resist: "A spell of indolence was upon him.... The thought passed dreamily through Aschenbach's brain that perhaps he had fallen into the clutches of a criminal; it had not power to rouse him to action" (*DV*, p. 22). Likewise, when he discovers that his trunk has been misdirected, he does not experience annoyance so much as a "reckless joy" that seems to be bound up with the oblivion of personal responsibility and the happiness of self-dispossession. Later we are told that Venice alone "had power to beguile him, to relax his resolution, to make him glad" (*DV*, p. 41). Indeed, the city itself seems to lure Aschenbach into self-abandon, as he begins to live only for Tadzio, following the family all over Venice, and even resting his head, one evening, on the boy's bedroom door: "It came at last to this—that his frenzy left him capacity for nothing else but to pursue his flame; to dream of him absent, to lavish, loverlike, endearing terms on his mere shadow" (*DV*, p. 56). By the close of *Death in Venice*, Aschenbach is quite overwhelmed by all of those *unreasonable* forces and aspects of himself that he had previously sought to suppress: his spiritual destruction is therefore complete.

Towards the end, Aschenbach has a dream which seems to measure exactly how far he has fallen:

> He trembled, he shrank, his will was steadfast to preserve and uphold his own god against this stranger who was sworn enemy to dignity and self-control. But the mountain wall took up the noise and howling and gave it back manifold; it rose high, swelled to a madness that carried him away. His senses reeled in the steam of panting bodies.... His heart throbbed to the drums, his brain reeled, a blind rage seized him, a whirling lust, he craved with all his soul to join the ring that formed about the obscene symbol of the godhead, which they were unveiling and elevating, monstrous and wooden, while from full throats they yelled their rallying cry. (*DV*, p. 68)

This is clearly a description of a Dionysian orgy, and it is based on Euripides' original depiction of this in *The Bacchae*. In Euripides' play, the ruler Pentheus is the champion of decency and self-control, who attacks Dionysus and will not recognize him as a god. In revenge, Dionysus makes him mad; by appealing to his curiosity, he tricks Pentheus into visiting the scene of the Dionysian orgy, where he is torn to pieces by Dionysus' followers. Just before he leaves, however, there is a very important scene in which Pentheus, now completely under Dionysus' spell, is persuaded to dress in women's clothing in order to visit the Bacchae undetected. This scene really represents Pentheus' final humiliation, since it was precisely his contempt and hatred for Dionysus as the effeminate "man-woman" that led him to see the latter as a threat to public decency in the first place. Significantly enough, there is a similar dressing scene in *Death in Venice* when Aschenbach goes to the hotel barber, having his hair dyed and his face rouged in order to look as young as possible for Tadzio. We are bound to recall the earlier incident on the ferry, when Aschenbach was totally repulsed by the appearance of the "old-young man" and the contemptible desire to pretend that one is much younger than one actually is. If Aschenbach now succumbs to the same temptation, we must regard it as his final degradation and humiliation, to be doing that which should disgust him more than anything else. But in this way, Dionysus the stranger-god punishes all those who deny him.

There is obviously a close parallel between Euripides' play and the progress of *Death in Venice*. Both works warn us of the dangers of rigid self-control and the refusal of the irrational part of our nature. And in this respect, it could be argued that both works offer a response to Plato's famous attack on poetry in the *Republic*. Here, in Book X of the *Republic* especially, Plato puts forward an ideal of rational self-constraint which allows him to condemn most poetry as a dangerous appeal to the unreasonable part of the soul. He only exempts "the unmixed imitation of the decent" as an acceptable way of promoting worthy ideals. In *Death in Venice*, Aschenbach serves as the representative of this "approved" kind of poetry insofar as his work confirms existing moral ideals and seems to threaten nothing. Nevertheless, such a stance leads to the disastrous explosion of his passionate nature. And from this it may be inferred that *Death in Venice* raises a profoundly anti-Platonic perspective.

—Richard White, "Love, Beauty, and Death in Venice." *Philosophy and Literature* 14, no. 1 (April 1990): pp. 56–58.

ROBERT TOBIN ON HOMOSEXUALITY

[Robert Tobin has been Professor of German at Whitman College in Walla Walla, Washington, since 1989. Author of *Warm Brothers: Queer Theory and the Age of Geothe* and *Doctor's Orders: Goethe and Enlightenment Thought*, he has also published essays on sexuality in the writings of Goethe and Mann. Here he asserts that several homoerotic encounters occur in the novella in addition to the ones between Aschenbach and Tadzio.]

Continuing to read experimentally, with an eye especially sensitive to gay themes, one could argue that, in wanting the "incomparable," Aschenbach wants the strange, i.e., the "queer" (13); in any case, he wants the "fabulously deviant," and he wants it "in a single night," stressing the nocturnal realm in which sexuality is at home (13). For Germans of Mann's era, the place to find such queerness was Italy, at least since Goethe made his erotic discoveries there and

Winckelmann moved there to lead his life more freely. In particular, Venice had become by the late nineteenth century a vacation center for homosexuals with means. Mann himself had played of this topos in an early story, "Disappointment," which describes a conversation between two solitary men in the Piazza San Marco of Venice; this can easily be read as a kind of attempted pick-up in which the cynicism and depression resulting from the clandestine lives of upper-class homosexuals in the late nineteenth century is discussed (Härle 168 ff.). Given this background, Aschenbach's desire to visit Venice is a logical extension of both his writing and his encounter with the stranger in the park.

In accordance with the homosexual aura surrounding Venice, a series of "queer" men accompany Aschenbach's arrival by sea to the fabled city. The first man, a "scruffy sailor" (13), leads Aschenbach to the salesman who sells him his ticket to Venice. This salesman speaks with "empty chatter" (14), echoing unflatteringly Aschenbach's protagonists, who, like Platen, rely on a highly formal textual style to confront their homosexuality. The next man on the way to Venice who suggests homosexuality is the fop who wears make-up in pretence of youth. His unpleasant behavior has explicit sexual overtones: "he . . . ran the tip of his tongue around the corners of his mouth in an obscenely suggestive manner" (16). Upon disembarking from the ship, he sends his compliments to "the beloved," using a suspiciously neuter noun in the German original, "Liebchen." The fourth character whose homosexuality sets the stage for events in Venice is the gondolier who, roughly but pleasantly, takes control of Aschenbach's life: "The smartest thing to do was to let matters take their course; more important, it was also the most pleasant" (19). The physical pleasure that Aschenbach takes in the actions of the strong man behind him has been seen by psychoanalysis as a wish for "a homosexual union" (Jofen 242). The disregarded anxiety that he may have fallen into the hands of a criminal reflects both the "dangerous life" of Aschenbach's heroes, the "born deceivers," and the actual life of homosexuals in the late nineteenth century, confined to dark corners and constantly endangered by blackmail. All of these "events of the journey that brought him here" cause Aschenbach to dwell on "the perverse . . . the forbidden" (21). Specifically, this perversity is "das Verkehrte," "wrong," but literally "backwards," "turned-around," referring to a tradition of seeing sodomy as sex on the wrong side, especially in this story, with its emphasis on "Verkehr," traffic and intercourse.

—Robert Tobin, "Why Is Tadzio a Boy?: Perspectives on Homoeroticism in Death in Venice." *Thomas Mann: Death in Venice*, trans. and ed. Clayton Koelb (New York: W.W. Norton, 1994): pp. 224–25.

Mario and the Magician

After he delivered his famous speech decrying nationalism in 1922, Mann would no longer be the apolitical figure he once stated he was. The 1930 publication of his allegory *Mario and the Magician* reflected his anxiety over the advancement of fascism in Europe. With a hypnotist's performance as its set piece, the novella presents an extended metaphor of fascism, referring in particular to the dynamics between a totalitarian government and its citizenry.

The narrator, a typical father and husband from Vienna whose name remains unknown, begins his account recalling the discomfort he felt during a family vacation in southern Italy. He uses vivid imagery to describe the hot, bustling Torre di Venere, where his family faced "the shocking business" of Cipolla, the magician who brought their holiday to a disastrous end. Throughout the narration the father expresses regret over the poor decisions he made, the first of which was to arrive in town in the middle of August, the worst month of the year. With only a few northern European tourists there in addition to the family, the town does not appear welcoming to foreigners.

After checking into the Grand Hotel, the family is informed that they must change accommodations. The management explains that one of their guests, a member of Italian royalty, fears that she will catch the whooping cough from one of the children recovering from the illness. Begrudgingly, the family moves their things to the Casa Eleonora, run by the congenial Signora Angiolieri. During the first few days of the vacation the father is disappointed by Torre, complaining about its stifling hot weather and crowded beaches. The native vacationers exhibit a nationalistic feeling that perplexes the Viennese children, who fail to make friends on the beach. The father, taking on a superior attitude, explains to the children that the country is "passing through a certain stage, something rather like an illness."

Things turn worse after the parents allow their eight-year-old daughter to take off her bathing suit and rinse it in the water. Many people grow furious at the display of nudity, and one angry man complains to the city authorities, who levy the family a fine for their misconduct. Following the disaster at the beach, the family considers leaving. But when other Italian guests at their hotel show their support and denounce the offensive behavior of the beachgoers, the family is persuaded to stay.

One day the children learn about the magician Cipolla's performance scheduled for that evening, and they beg their parents to go. Despite the lateness of the event, the parents decide to indulge their children. The venue turns out to be tucked away in the city's alleys, and mostly local people are in attendance, some of whom the family has gotten to know during their stay. Signora Angiolieri and her husband are there, and so is Mario, a sensitive, reserved teenager who works at a café the family has frequented. After a long delay, Cavaliere Cipolla finally emerges onto the stage. He is an older man with a "sharp, ravaged face," and is deformed by a hump in his lower back. Instead of a wand he carries a whip, which he uses frequently, and he sustains his waning energy through the performance by drinking cognac.

Cipolla faces his audience in a serious and haughty manner, which invites an early taunt from a brash youth in the crowd. The magician responds by humiliating the boy, conjuring him with the snap of his whip to stick out his tongue to the audience. After putting the boy in his place, Cipolla gives some background on himself, describing his great performances of the past. He also explains his source of strength as a magician: "It is perforce with my mental and spiritual parts that I conquer life—which after all only means conquering oneself." The narrator observes that the magician's eloquent words, in addition to his recent trick, have impressed a good portion of the audience already. The people are also impressed by the sacrifices Cipolla attests to make to perform his tricks. When he hypnotizes people, he claims that the effect is just as debilitating on him as it is on the entranced. In the minds of his naive audience, Cipolla sacrifices himself for the good of entertainment, just as, in the minds of many Europeans of this era, fascist leaders sacrificed themselves for the good of the nation.

After his long introduction, Cipolla invites two teenagers to participate in an arithmetic trick on a blackboard onstage. The two boys confess that they do not know how to write the figures that Cipolla calls out, which the magician believes is pitiful. He launches into a sermon about how every Italian should be able to write, which compels the victim of Cipolla's first trick to stand again and defend the boys onstage. The magician humiliates the boy for the second time, conjuring him to bend over and demonstrate a sudden case of colic. Over the course of Cipolla's performance, the narrator begins to perceive the dynamics between the magician and his audience. For the reader, there are clear parallels between these dynamics and the dynamics of a fascist system. For instance, while the magician is not popular, he is compelling enough that the audience remains passive and courteous; and with his whip, he has the ever-present threat of force to achieve his goals.

The intermission presents the father with an opportunity to leave. He knows the hour is very late and the children have long been asleep, yet he decides to stay, admitting that he has no sensible reason to do so. "Again, sheer curiosity may account for something," he explains with regret. The second half of the performance begins with Cipolla hypnotizing Signora Angiolieri into following him around the room. Even when Cipolla asks her husband to call her back to her seat, she remains under the spell until the hypnotist snaps his whip to bring her back into consciousness. He then hypnotizes several others to dance wildly on the stage. As a final triumph, he sets a strong-willed Roman gentleman dancing with the others. As the crowd falls into a frenzy, the father watches his children's elation at the spectacle. He realizes with dismay that they are oblivious to the awful nature of Cipolla's power.

For the final trick of the evening, Cipolla calls the timid Mario to the stage. From another boy in the crowd, Cipolla ascertains the name of a girl, Silvestra, with whom Mario is smitten. The boy is hypnotized into thinking that Cipolla is Silvestra. The magician asks for a kiss on the cheek, and after the entranced boy does as requested, the crowd erupts with laughter. Mario becomes frantic, pulls out a gun, and fires two bullets into Cipolla. The old man slips off his chair and dies, after which several crowd members quickly disarm and apprehend Mario.

The narrator rushes his family out of the room. The children, oblivious to the tragedy that has just occurred, ask if the show has ended. The father assures them that it has, and at the same he tries to convince himself that the horror has ended as well. With this catastrophe lingering so long in his memory, it is clear that for him the horror is not over, a fact that makes the story's conclusion all the more harrowing.

Mario and the Magician

The narrator recounts the ill-fated magic performance during a summer vacation with his family. Offended by the nationalistic fervor of some of the Italians, he considers leaving early, but to his later regret he decides against it. During the performance he has every intention to take his children away from the scene, but he remains entranced by the magician's power and passive to his oppressive tactics.

Cavaliere Cipolla is the aging, hunchbacked hypnotist who dominates his audience through magic, willpower, and manipulation. He wins the sympathy of the weak-willed and through humiliation, subjugates the strong. With his power tactics and his allegiance to the "Fatherland," he serves as an analogue to the fascist leaders of the period.

Mario is a sensitive, young waiter at a café the narrator's family frequents during their vacation. After Cipolla hypnotizes Mario into kissing him on the cheek, he shoots and kills the magician.

Sofronia Angiolieri is the proprietress of the hotel where the narrator's family stays. She is also hypnotized by Cipolla, who makes her follow him completely around the room.

The brash youth is the first to stand up to Cipolla and the first to fall under his hypnotic powers, after which few audience members attempt to challenge the magician's authority.

The Roman gentleman boasts that Cipolla cannot hypnotize him against his will. His failure to resist Cipolla, who sets him into a wild dance, marks the magician's final triumph over the crowd.

Mario and the Magician

HENRY C. HATFIELD ON FASCISM

[Henry C. Hatfield was Senior Research Professor of German at Harvard University and general editor of the *Germanic Review*. His scholarly works include *Thomas Mann* and *Goethe: A Critical Introduction*. In this extract he compares the tricks of the magician Cipolla with the tactics of the fascist leaders of Mann's time.]

In 1930 Mann was to deliver his first major attack on Nazism: *Appeal to Reason*. The point of view of this speech has much in common with that of *Mario*. In both there is the combination of patrician scorn for fascism with the almost incredulous realization that it must be taken seriously.

It is in the appearance and character of Cipolla that the political implications of the novella are most clearly brought out. Again and again he has recourse to two great sources of power in carrying out his magic: the claw-handled whip and the stimulus of cognac. Force and fraud, as it were; and Mann draws our attention to these symbols with almost Wagnerian insistence. Cipolla is a mixture of apparently contradictory traits; he looks like a "charlatan and mountebank," a veritable Cagliostro; yet like the *petite bourgeoisie* on the beach he is completely devoid of humor. He is grotesque and ridiculous, but one does not feel like laughing at him. There is something almost fantastically old-fashioned about his dress. (In the essays and speeches in which Mann warned the Germans of the implications of fascism, it was precisely its reactionary, "old-fashioned" character which he stressed.) Like the fascist leaders, he deliberately appears late before his audience, and he displays the striped sash of a highly dubious nobility.

The magician speaks with such brilliant eloquence that he gains the grudging respect of the uneasy listeners. There is in him a curious combination of boastfulness and self-pity; he claims that it is he, not his victims, who suffers during his feats of hypnotism. He paints himself, in other words, as the all-wise, all-enduring hero, the leader of the people. Arrogance predominates in his character, but it is an obvious compensation for ugliness and deformity; his sensitiveness about "national honor" repeats that of the bowler-hatted man on the beach. Indeed, Cipolla's chauvinism is such that he does not shrink from the most obviously absurd lies: "In Italy, everybody can write." Just before he is killed, he shows a strong homosexual tendency, a tendency for which the German fascists were already notorious. Above all: one must not underrate the magician's powers; he gradually reveals himself as "the most powerful hypnotist I have ever seen in my life." (One remembers that he had billed himself as a mere prestidigitator.)

At least one critic conceives of the magician as another of those "marked men" whom Mann delights to describe. In this view, he would be but another of the symbols of the artist, a relative, as it were, of Tonio Kröger, Gustave Aschenbach, Felix Krull and all the others. This interpretation seems to rest on the unflattering assumption that there is only a single theme in all Mann's work, that of the lonely and maladjusted artist. Seen in this way, *Mario* loses its individuality and becomes a sort of "*Death in Venere*." But Cipolla, for all of his occult powers, is no artist. He lacks the all-important trait which, in Mann's view, distinguishes the creator: a frustrated and at times scornful love for ordinary humanity, for the "blond and blue-eyed."

In his handling of the audience, Cipolla is a master of demagogic tactics. Divide and rule is his method, and he uses it with supreme skill. Before his performance starts, he is challenged by a brash youth; by hypnotic powers the magician makes him insult the rest of the audience. He reduces another youth, significantly enough, to a state of "military somnambulism." At first Cipolla leaves the better-dressed spectators alone, concentrating on those whom ignorance or lack of self-assurance render vulnerable. To break down the barrier between the leader and the masses he leaves the platform and circulates among the audience. Finally the aristocrats, including an army officer, a lady of cultural pretensions, and even a "long-toothed Anglo-Saxoness" fall under his spell. By flattery, tricks, intimidation, and above all by hypnotic powers of whose genuineness the author leaves no doubt, Cipolla subdues practically the entire audience.

At one point he assumes a seemingly passive role, performing prodigies of mind-reading in obedience to the will of the spectators. The leader must be able to sense what his people desires. But Cipolla makes it clear that his will is still dominant after all. His remarks about the unity of commanding and obeying and the oneness of the leader and the people sound like direct quotations from some work of fascist dogma.

The audience, it is worth stressing, has never liked the magician. Its attitude towards him is shifting and ambivalent, and generally it shows sympathy for his victims. Yet no one leaves the performance; Cipolla exudes a fascination as a person, "independently of the program." A new theme is established: this is a story of the will, as well as of fascism; or rather, the two elements, moral and political tyranny, are closely interrelated and finally fused into one.

—Henry C. Hatfield, "Mario and the Magician." *The Stature of Thomas Mann*, (New York: New Directions, 1947): pp. 170–71.

ALLAN J. MCINTYRE ON DETERMINISM

[Allan J. McIntyre taught in the Modern Languages department at the University of Akron, Ohio, and has published essays on European literature in the *Germanic Review*. In this excerpt he observes the story from a deterministic perspective and argues that Cipolla is not the real enemy.]

The greatest irony in the prolonged contest of wills between Cipolla and resisting members of his audience, including the passive resistance of the storyteller, lies in the fact, as we have seen, that the tug-of-war is basically an illusion, for its course and result are determined by causal factors external to and independent of any principle of final autonomy in individuals. The fate which overtakes the magician is conveyed by Mann with the overpowering sense that it is ultimately the result of an impersonal shifting of mighty weights, which yet serves justice, as in a great mill grinding small, or better, given its suddenness, like the slipping of a ship's cargo in a gale, a cargo critically poised from the start of the voyage, with the crumpled human form of the magician on the stage at the close, reduced to mere debris, as mute testimony to the fact that he was in the way.

This revelation of emptiness at the heart of power leads to a consideration of the author's attitude toward the creature whom he has portrayed without a single redeeming, let alone endearing trait. On the level of determinism, apart from the grotesque and hateful manifestations of his personality, Cipolla is a pitiful character, and the reader senses that the large sympathy of a creator, who sees the problematical in everything, may not be entirely withheld even from him, although the strictures of the story may preclude an overt expression. After all, there can be nothing tragic about an arch villain and his just deserts, unless one can see him, too, somehow, as a victim. The last words of the storyteller provide a clue. Insisting on the liberating, cathartic effects of Cipolla's death, he says: "ich konnte und kann nicht umhin, es so zu empfinden," by this comparative vehemence drawing the reader's attention once more to the enormity of the deterministic process which has caused it. Having grasped that process, we understand with the author that Cipolla simply had to be eliminated, but the knowledge is a sobering one. This ending has brought us full circle to the fateful remark at the beginning of the story, only now a slightly different flavor is conveyed in these last expostulatory and somewhat agitated words of a man who has witnessed a terrible thing. A trace of pity seems to hang on the air. In this regard, it may be recalled that the humanist exile from his own land, Thomas Mann, was one who could write a probing essay on a subject he execrated, and entitle it, characteristically, "Bruder-Hitler."

—Allan J. McIntyre, "Determinism in *Mario and the Magician.*" *Germanic Review* 52, no. 3 (May 1977): pp. 215–16.

TERRI APTER ON POWER DYNAMICS

[Terri Apter is Senior Tutor at Newnham College of Cambridge University. Her critical works include *Thomas Mann: The Devil's Advocate, Virginia Woolf: A Study of Her Novels,* and *Fantasy Literature: An Approach to Reality.* In this excerpt from her book on Mann, she focuses on the fatal naïveté of the audience and the overwhelming power of Cipolla, who represents the archetypal artist.]

The magician is a hybrid of the artist and politician. His purpose as mass hypnotiser is not camouflaged by the aura of a political campaign nor is his mass vision decorated by artistic taste. He represents, starkly, in its nastiest aspect, the malevolent power of the artist's sensibility.

The drama of *Mario and the Magician*, like that of *Death in Venice*, is embedded within the atmospheric setting. In many respects the atmosphere is similar to that of the earlier novella for the tale takes place in an Italian seaside resort with a heat that breeds both indolence and wildness; but whereas the debilitation and corruption of Venice mark a spiritual or imaginative striving that has failed, Torre di Venere wallows in the vulgar and the banal. Illbred merrymakers, with full-throated, hideously stressed cries, crowd the beach and cafés. The German family is not seduced by beauty but by the coarse and the commonplace. Inert and fascinated, they remain at the resort despite the cheap upsurge of national fervour which expresses itself as hostility towards foreigners. The German family believe that in staying they are facing up to life's difficulties, that they are exhibiting admirable resolution, but this moral stance is only a subterfuge for their attraction to the sinister atmosphere.

The sinister is magnetic, but it has none of the lush sense of promise that dwelt within Aschenbach's degrading visions. However repulsive the object, the magician can make it desirable: this is the point and horror of the tale. Freedom does not lie in the ability to carry out the impulses of the will, for the will is subject to the crudest influences and delusions. The magician Cipolla persuades his audience to act according to their will, and he proves that such 'freedom' disgusts them. Sipping cognac, smoking the cheapest brand of cigarettes and exhaling the smoke through his rotting teeth, looking like a circus director with his foppish air and black-varnished, frizzled hair, he preys upon people's hidden desires and frustrations, and uses this sympathy to manipulate them. The audience pities the youth upon whom Cipolla first excercises his power, for the youth appears to be in convulsions of pain; but Cipolla tells his audience that he himself is the one in pain, and that the youth is simply expressing what the magician actually feels. Cipolla so keenly sympathises with those people over whom he exercises his power that he himself is burdened by their feelings. His power, though obviously malevolent, has an aspect of loving patronage; his manipulation is a sympathetic participation in the people's will.

Cipolla's audience is slow to understand that the magician's stunts are more than a game, that they are truly his subjects, and that their wills can be so easily touched by the will of another. Innocence is no protection against such influences. The children of the German couple find Cipolla's stunts inexpressibly delightful; innocence applauds this evil, finding it a marvellous entertainment. Cipolla, as artist-tyrant, can captivate the pious and ethereal Signora Angioliere. She would follow him to the ends of the earth, while her husband's voice, the voice of love and duty, remains unheard. She beholds in the vulgar, deformed magician the realisation of her highest dreams, just as the audience in *Felix Krull* saw in Müller-Rosé their heart's desire; but the magician works directly upon the will; he does not captivate by beauty or by any other means that contain something of value. He is pure power, and purely revolting. Cipolla convinces the waiter Mario—the man whose duty is to serve and who therefore serves the magician's will—that he, the foul-breathed old man, is the infinitely desirable Sylvestra, and Mario passionately kisses the magician. Realising his mistake, realising that his senses can be totally at odds with his soul's desire, Mario shoots the magician. The narrator admits that he is relieved to see the magician dead, for he has witnessed the horrific effect of a man who persuades the people to act according to their will.

The will cannot be taught to discriminate either beauty from ugliness or good from evil: that is the pessimistic message of this tale. The tension between life and imagination is no longer the dominant theme; the problem is life's use of imagination.

—T. E. Apter, *Thomas Mann: The Devil's Advocate*, (New York: New York University Press, 1979): pp. 136–38.

SIEGFRIED MANDEL ON FREUD AND NIETZSCHE

[Siegfried Mandel is Professor of English and Comparative Literature at the University of Colorado–Boulder. He has translated into English many works by German essayist Lou Andreas Salomé, and is author of *Nietzsche and the Jews: Exaltation and Denigration* and *Rainer Maria Rilke: The*

Poetic Instinct. Here he illustrates the influence of Freud's and Nietzsche's ideas on the story.]

The psychological allusions, I believe, determine the vital thrust of the novella. During the Twenties, the philosophical influence of Nietzsche's ideas about the primacy of the will—and the antithesis between life and intellect—and Schopenhauer's ideas of the world as will and representation that had informed Mann's earlier works began to subside or merge with his increased fascination with the dynamics of mythical-psychological thought. Most instructive are Mann's essays of which he said that "they are fated to accompany or to act as a critique upon my own creative work." And so, Mann's first lecture essay on Freud, delivered in Munich on May 16, 1929, has a direct bearing upon the Joseph novel which was in progress and upon *Mario and the Magician.* Called *"Die Stellung Freuds in der modernen Geistesgeschichte"* ("Freud's Position in the History of Modern Thought," *Past Masters* [1933; rpt. New York: Books for Library Press, 1968]), the essay includes sharp criticism of contemporaneous political trends. Mann cites an early study by Nietzsche, *Menschliches, Allzumenschliches,* in which the philosopher refers to "the appearance of certain powerful and irresistible spirits, who yet are reactionary and invoke a past epoch, as indicating that the new orientation is not yet strong enough to oppose them successfully." Cipolla, in part, is representative of the reactionary forces that distort and allude to glories of the past, whereas humanistic forces of which Freud is a new and revolutionary interpreter are incipient; only the revolutionary really understands and knows how to tap the thoughts of antiquity. Although Mann's use of "reaction" and "progress" is complicated and suggests a symbiotic relationship, he dramatizes unambiguously in *Mario and the Magician* the contrast between fascism's manipulation of myth and Freud's humanization of it.

Mann's interest in the mythological-psychological deepened upon reading Freud's *Totem and Taboo.* There he saw analogies between the primitive and the modern, as well as what might be prehistorical residues in the modern psyche. Mann speaks of Freud's "inexorable surgeon's probe" into the "horrifying and culturally fecund, morbid world of incest dread . . . and murder remorse," the psychology of instinct—"the night side of nature and the soul"—the primacy of the unconscious, the pre-mental, the will as against passion or, "as Nietzsche said the 'feeling above the reason.'" In substance, *Mario and the Magician* unfolds the mainsprings of passion, the irrational, and the demonicism of the unconscious in reaction to conscious will, reason, and intellect. The antirationalistic interpretations of psychoanalysis intrigued Mann: "'As a psychoanalyst,' Freud takes occasion to say in a little autobiographical sketch, 'I must of course be more interested in affective than in intellectual phenomena; more in the unconscious than in the conscious mental life.' An extremely simple sentence, but full of meaning . . . the calm allusion to 'unconscious mental life.'" In addition to the concepts of repression, sublimation, and the unconscious, Freud noted the phenomenon of transference in which the patient pours out his unconscious fears, hostilities, and hidden affections and transfers them to the analyst. Cipolla triggers such transference by Mario, with fatal consequences for himself. In his later essay, *Freud and the Future* (1937), Mann came to regard "psychology as truth in the essential and most courageous sense."

—Siegfried Mandel, "Mann's *Mario and the Magician*, Or Who Is Silvestra?" *Modern Fiction Studies* 25, no. 4 (Winter 1979–80): pp. 600–601.

DAGMAR BARNOUW ON THE STORY'S MESSAGE

[Dagmar Barnouw is Professor of German and Comparative Literature at the University of Southern California. His books include *Weimar Intellectuals and the Threat of Modernity* and a book analyzing Mann's writings. In this extract he investigates the story's connection between art and politics.]

The plot and the narrative success of *Mario and the Magician* turns on the tension, seductively strong and little affected by the familiar irony, between desire and betrayal, between the naive fragmentation of life and the cunning perfectionism of art. Many readers have found this tension the most plausible and also most easily recognized access to the text. But even then, the story contains clearly contradictory messages about its meaning, and the most ambiguous one concerns the role played by contemporary politics in Mann's re-writing a particular experience in this particular way. The challenge to the reader, then, seems not so much the extraction of the text's core-message regarding political-historical events. It seems, rather, the detection of these events' ambiguous presence in the construct of the story.

Yet (professional) readers have tended to circumvent this challenge. Consider for instance the argument that "the magician's inability to understand the [Italian] national heritage in its full significance ultimately costs him his power and his life." Schwarz reasons that in underestimating the danger Mario poses to him, Cipolla does not take seriously the heroic *and* the Republican connotations in the culturally important tradition of Marius. This reading is given high praise in Vaget's *Thomas Mann—Kommentar*, especially in connection with Schwarz' emphasis on the almost prophetic decisiveness of Mann's showing the necessarily violent end of the rule of fascism. But the act of violence in the story is intimately connected with the a-historical, the artistic demonization of fascism pointed out by Schwarz himself. The text is much too slippery to carry the general message about a resistance to fascism supported by an Italian cultural tradition. Cipolla dies because of Mann's authorial decision. It was the construct of the story that required the change from the passivity of the real-life waiter of Mann's acquaintance, which that young man shared with a majority of Italians and Germans under totalitarian rule, to the neatly decisive act of his fictional counterpart.

There is another attempt at a clean solution of troubling textual ambiguities in McIntyre's essay about the story's "determinism." In killing Cipolla, he argues, Mario is nothing but "the simple instrument of a poetic justice." But he then proceeds to connect both Mario's instrumentality and Cipolla's demonic artistry with the influence on Mann of Schopenhauer's concept of the will: "There is no doubt that Cipolla is the master of a demonic art, with a hypnotic personality of the first order. It must be clear, however, that because he is an incorporation, indeed almost the caricature of Will, his actions must be completely determined thereby, and therefore he is a slave, not a master." This inversion allows McIntyre to account for the equation of art and political "evil" *without* having to consider the cultural implications of such equation. But the very forcefulness of this inversion suggests that the text's play on control, affirming a linkage between the perfectionism of art and totalitarian rule, is not contained so easily.

> —Dagmar Barnouw, "Fascism, Modernity, and the Doctrine of Art from *Mario and the Magician* to *Doctor Faustus.*" *Michigan Germanic Studies* 28, no. 1 (Spring 1992): pp. 54–55.

MARTIN TRAVERS ON THE AUTHOR'S POLITICS

[Martin Travers is Senior Lecturer in the School of Humanities at Griffith University in Queensland, Australia, and is author of *An Introduction to Modern European Literature* and *Thomas Mann*, an analysis of the author's writings. In this excerpt from that book, Travers places the story in the context of Mann's stance against Nazi Germany.]

The speech 'German Address: A Call to Reason' represents, however, more than just a call to action; it also offers an analysis of the techniques employed by the Nazis to reach their goals. The Nazis have won success so far because they have, with great psychological insight and the most sophisticated employment of propaganda techniques, produced a style of politics that thrives on 'wild, confusing effects, [which are] at one and the same time, nervous, enervating and intoxicating'. Their fascist brand of politics cannot be explained simply as a reflex of class allegiance or economic interest; it is also a 'psychic disposition', something that draws upon and appeals to 'unconscious forces' within the individual: fears and insecurities, but also wish-fulfilments and phantasies. It succeeds because it appeals, not to reason, but to the irrational, to unreason. The natural ally of the educated middle-class, Mann concludes, is not the extreme Right but the moderate Left, represented by the Social Democrats, who are the sole bearers of the liberal traditions of freedom and democracy.

Mann's speculations about the mechanics of fascist politics provide an important context for one of his major works of fiction of this period: the novella *Mario and the Magician*, published just prior to the speech in 1930. At first sight, the story seems to have little to do with the contemporary state of German politics, or with politics in general. It tells of how a German family on holiday at an Italian sea-side resort come to be bewitched and then horrified by the exploits of Cipolla—a magician cum hypnotist, during one of his evening performances. *Mario and the Magician* takes up a number of themes common in Mann's work, such as the moral ambiguity of art and the artist and the unbridgeable gulf between artist and society to which this leads, but Mann treats these themes in such a way that they become open to political interpretation. For Cipolla is no ordinary stage magician; he is a highly adept hypnotist, whose total control over his audience is made possible by the existence of exactly the same sorts of physic forces, those 'powers stronger than reason or virtue', that demagogues such as Hitler were able to manipulate. It is for this reason that *Mario the Magician* might well be termed a study in the psychology of fascist politics. Cipolla, the 'magician', stands in the same relation to his audience as the fascist politician stands in relation to the crowd at a political rally: both treat their 'audiences' as the passive objects of an elaborate process of manipulation, and both draw on the same techniques to achieve their nefarious goals: intimidation, bluff, brow beating and a mixed bag of 'artistic' tricks and technical illusionism.

—Martin Travers, "The Call to Unreason: *Mario and the Magician.*" *Thomas Mann*, (New York: St. Martin's Press, 1992): pp. 76–77.

EVA GEULEN ON TOTALITARIANISM

[Eva Geulen is Associate Professor of German Languages and Literature at New York University. Her writings include essays on Theodor Adorno, Friedrich Nietzsche, Walter Benjamin, and Thomas Mann. Here she reflects on the interactions between Cipolla and his audience, which in turn sheds light on the dynamics between the author and the reader.]

This text—ostensibly about an individual, desperate act of radical resistance to an intentionally allegorized fascism—is a text about resistance in all too many senses and all too many ways. It begins with the narrator's passive resistance, his "constancy" (143) and "inertia" (165) which resists the inclination to leave the inhospitable place, and it ends with the rather more aggressive resistance of Mario's shots. All instances of resistance, those represented and those operative in the mode of representation, obey the rule that resistance is complicitous. And because everything in this text depends on a narrator who is as susceptible to complicity with fascist modes of thought as the audience is susceptible to Cipolla's seductions, any distinction between what is represented and the mode of representation is problematic. The text thus remains in the same ambivalence that characterizes Cipolla's performance; both leave one wondering, "where the comedy left off and the tragedy began" (133). Perhaps aware of this quality of the text as a whole, Mann himself expressed hesitant ambivalence as to the politics of this piece, which is usually characterized as yet another milestone in the author's supposedly exemplary metamorphosis from the apolitical German to the antifascist defender of democratic virtues. Mann, however, wavered between attributing to it antifascist intentions and locating it in the more general realm of the ethical.

For quite some time this ambivalence found expression in two different categories of the reception. Analysis characteristically would focus either on the general psychological dynamics and the poetic technique or on decoding the novella's political symbolism. Indeed, entire theories of fascism were verified on the basis of this text, from the analysis of Mann's carefully choreographed class relations to a reading of the theatrical nature of the performer as a case of fascist aestheticization of politics and psychological speculations on the dialectic of sadism and masochism in mass seduction. The changes within the political interpretations roughly correspond to the changes in general theories of fascism. Mann's text has been rich enough to accommodate all of them with varying degrees of persuasiveness. Still, Mario no longer figures today as the working-class hero who breaks the spell of ideology (as he did for Lukács), nor are the spectators just innocent victims of nameless evil and demonic seduction. For the precarious complicity of the narrator with Cipolla becomes legible, at the latest, when one reads that he "involuntarily made with [his] lips the sound that Cipolla's whip had made when it cut the air" (150).

As more and more such instances of complicity were discovered, the mode of representation came into view as a function of such complicity, mainly through the figure of the narrator. His condescending attitude—the Italian middle class is figured as "human mediocrity and middle-class scum"—and blatantly racist convictions, which come to the fore when he alludes to the prevailing nationalistic atmosphere as a relapse from European civilization into African primitivity, is certainly of a kind with the fascist ideology that is supposedly the object of critique.

Such incidents of "entanglement" are not just thematic nor merely incidental but find systematic expression in the narrative technique, for the narrator's strategies are modeled on Cipolla's own. While the latter works from the start "to eliminate the gap between stage and audience" (153), the narrator addresses his readers through a number of excursions and apostrophes. The two part structure of the magic show corresponds to the two part narrative. Strategic delays to increase the tension belong to the repertoire of the narrator as much as to Cipolla's. That the tactics resemble each other so strongly should come as no surprise. Both magicians—Mann was known within his family as the magician—excel in linguistic eloquence: "*parla benissimo!*" (151) While the narrator becomes a victim of one performer, so the reader becomes a victim of the other. Since the story is told from hindsight but does not reveal the end of the plot until the end of the narrative, the reader is placed into a strangely complicitous position. As a representation, the text reenacts the very performance it represents in the mode of representation. The narrative is as much about performance as it is itself performative. The narrator's conjecture, "that all this was part of the show—the analphabetic yokels no less than the giovanotto with the jacket" (155), is equally applicable to his own theatrical performance.

—Eva Geulen, "Resistance and Representation: A Case Study of Thomas Mann's *Mario and the Magician.*" *New German Critique* 68 (1996): pp. 16–18.

PLOT SUMMARY OF

"Disorder and Early Sorrow"

Written in 1925, "Disorder and Early Sorrow" is a portrait of a middle-class family during the inflation years following World War I. Told from the point of view of Abel Cornelius, a pensive history professor and father of four, the story offers a detailed perspective on domestic life in Germany during this time. Over the course of a typical day, Cornelius appears to us initially as a content and satisfied father, but his feelings of powerlessness in a changing world gradually intensify until the story's poignant conclusion.

The reader is introduced to the family members as they prepare a party for the teenage children and their friends. The narrator divides the family into four age groups, with teenagers Bert and Ingrid as the "Big Folk," Cornelius and his wife as the "Old Folk," the grandparents as the "Ancient Folk," and the two young children as the "Little Folk." The young boy, Snapper, is the mother's favorite child, while the five-year-old Ellie is Cornelius' favorite. With her charming ways, Ellie elicits an uncharacteristic delight from the normally gloomy professor. It is her "early sorrow" that is the source of his imminent grief.

The inflation has demanded of the family many changes, of which the story offers several instances. The house has been for some time in need of repairs, and everyone is forced to wear worn clothing, a sacrifice that fortunately does not upset the children. Frau Cornelius, wearied from having to do her own housekeeping, has become especially frugal with the family's resources. Not all the changes, however, seem this drastic, or even necessary. Cornelius, for example, recently decided to shave his pointed beard as a "concession to the changing times."

While his wife and children make preparations for the party, Cornelius follows his daily routine, first reviewing for the next day's lecture. While working out his lesson plan, he meditates on his own view of the historical past, which he believes has an order and permanence that the modern age is missing. He treasures his feelings for his innocent daughter Ellie, feelings also arising from his love for order and permanence.

Cornelius takes his daily nap and by the time he wakes up, the party has begun. He goes downstairs and Ingrid introduces him to their friends, among them Max Hergesell, an upstanding, eager-to-please engineering student, and Ivan Herzl, an artist-type who wears rouge. Cornelius is troubled about Ivan's rouge, as he is with a number of other peculiarities he observes about Bert and Ingrid's generation.

Cornelius, noticeably self-conscious around his guests, retreats to his study again, but his thoughts remain on the party. He returns to the drawing room when he hears that one of the guests has picked up his guitar and begun singing folk songs. Although he notices that the boy "obviously neither owns nor cares to own the correct evening dress of the middle classes," Cornelius appreciates his presence and envies him because he has the admirable qualities that his son Bert is missing. Cornelius often indicates his disappointment in Bert, who reflects the disorder of the times with his disheveled appearance and idle ways.

When the guests begin to dance, the servants come out from the kitchen to watch. Among them are the Hinterhofer sisters, who regret that they no longer belong to the middle class. Both sisters affect a wounded pride, and one refuses to wear a cap "or other badge of servitude." Like Bert, the lazy manservant Xaver is a "product of the disrupted times," with dubious dreams of becoming a movie star.

At one point Cornelius approaches Ellie, who is entranced by the music and pays no attention to her father. The snub Cornelius receives from her instills in him a sudden hatred for the party and its effect on his little daughter. He tells his wife that he believes it is time for the younger children to go to bed, and he leaves the room to go for his nightly walk. Once out of the house, he becomes preoccupied again with his teaching, focusing on the approach he feels he must take with the younger generation. He reminds himself that it is not prudent to take sides on political issues because it only causes more conflict and scandal. One must be impartial, he believes, in order to live in accordance with the ordered past.

Upon returning to the house, Cornelius learns that Ellie has become inconsolably upset. When he finds her in her room, he is so dismayed by his daughter's crying that he turns on the servants, accusing them of causing her misery. He eventually learns from Ellie that she has a crush on the older Max, and that she could not stand having to leave him to go to bed. Though still dismayed, he is secretly happy that she has turned to him in a time of need, and that his role as her consoling father is still secure.

Meanwhile, Xaver has found Max and brought him to Ellie in the hopes that a formal good-night will pacify her. Max graciously does his duty, and the girl is restored to her joyful self again. Cornelius reacts to the boy's kind gesture with an intriguing mixture of "thankfulness, embarrassment, and hatred." The scene reminds Cornelius of a maudlin tale in which a dying child asks to see a clown, and once the clown appears, the child dies happy. Cornelius then says good night to Ellie, and as she falls asleep, he marvels that her longing for Max will be entirely forgotten by the morning.

The story's final scene reveals how much the present world troubles Cornelius, and how much he relies on the innocent perspective of his daughter. "How good that she breathes in oblivion with every breath she draws!" he observes as she watches her sleep. Her memory is easily wiped clean, unlike his own, with its stubborn longing for the past.

"Disorder and Early Sorrow"

Abel Cornelius is the head of the family and the central figure of the story. An introspective professor longing for the golden past, he reacts to the changes of the times with apprehension, and finds his only real comfort in the naive perspective of his young daughter.

Ellie is the five-year-old daughter who during the party becomes enamored with one of the teenage guests, Max Hergesell. She suffers her first heartbreak when she is forced to part with him at the end of the night.

Ingrid is the lively, teenage daughter who arranges the evening party. She idly spends much of her free time with Bert making crank calls and doing impersonations of common people.

Bert, a blond 17-year-old, has aspirations to become a Cabaret performer. In Cornelius' eyes, his disheveled style and carefree bearing gives him an appearance similar to the servant's.

Max Hergesell is an upstanding engineering student and the object of Ellie's early crush. His charming effect on the young girl arouses Cornelius' envy.

Frau Cornelius is run down by having to do her own housekeeping during the inflation, but she has adapted well to the current food shortages.

Xaver Kleinsgutl is the feckless young servant of the household. His poor work habit proves him to be, in Cornelius' words, a "child and product of the disrupted times."

Ivan Herzl is a student of modern theatre and friend of Bert and Ingrid. His eccentric style and its influence on Bert are a source of anxiety for Cornelius.

Snapper is the young four-year-old son with sensitive nerves, another purported effect of the times. He is also Frau Cornelius' favorite child.

"Disorder and Early Sorrow"

IGNACE FEUERLICHT ON THE STORY'S INCEPTION

[Ignace Feuerlicht taught at State University of New York–New Paltz. He is author of *Alienation: From the Past to the Future* and a book on Mann's fiction. This extract from his book on Mann offers an overview of the story's major themes along with an explanation of its inception.]

"Disorder and Early Sorrow" (1925) is one of Mann's most popular stories. He "improvised it for relaxation" after the long and strenuous work on *The Magic Mountain* and published it in *Die Neue Rundschau* on the occasion of his fiftieth birthday. The "early sorrow" is felt by the five-year old Ellie. Max Hergesell, 'a pleasant and good-looking student, has jocularly danced with her at the house party and she cannot stop crying or fall asleep until Max visits her in her bedroom. The "disorder" is the inflation, the postwar shortages and privations, the way of life of the young generation in Germany, specifically in Munich, around 1922 and 1923. To the professor, his feelings for his daughter Ellie represent order and timelessness among the disorder, lawlessness, and irrelevance of his time, but Ellie herself seems to be seized by the very "disorder."

Dr. Cornelius has pangs of jealousy because his little daughter, whom he loves above everything, has "fallen in love" with another man. He also feels out of place in the postwar world. While the young enjoy the present and look forward to the future, he is immersed in the past, not only because of his age but also because he is a professor of history, whose "heart belongs to the coherent and disciplined historic past" (506). Ironically, the whole novella, which is told from the professor's point of view, is narrated in the present tense. Yet, Mann had just finished *The Magic Mountain*, which calls the narrator the "conjurer of the past tense."

Dr. Cornelius is, of course, Mann himself, who had a professorial appearance and bent. Eleanor is Mann's favorite child Elisabeth. The other Cornelius children, Ingrid, Bert, and Snapper, resemble

Erika, Klaus, and Michael Mann. The ages of the members of the Mann family and those of their equivalents in the Cornelius family are identical. Contrary to her role in *Royal Highness*, but in line with "Mario and the Magician," Katja Mann is not much in evidence.

The ambitions, successes, failures, jokes, slang, dances, and peculiarities of the young men and women (students, actors, employees, and servants), the gulf between the generations, the devaluation of the money and of the bourgeois tradition, parental love and worries, and, above all, the behavior of little children are rendered with skill, charm, and humor, with malice toward none and gentle irony toward all. Mann escaped the Scylla of bitterness and the Charybdis of sentimentality. The professor is no pedant, and even those readers who find Mann ponderous in his great works take delight in this professorial sketch.

—Ignace Feuerlicht, *Thomas Mann*, (Boston: Twayne Publishers, 1968): pp. 143–44.

Franklin E. Court on False Appearances

[Franklin E. Court is a former Professor of English at Northern Illinois University and author of *The Scottish Connection: The Rise of English Literary Study in Early America* and *Institutionalizing English Literature: The Culture and Politics of Literary Study*. Here he discusses how the story portrays deception through its characterizations and various motifs.]

Professor Cornelius's loss of his young daughter, Ellie, and Ellie's loss of Max Hergesell, the "fairy prince" who captures her tiny heart at the "big folks'" party in Mann's "Disorder and Early Sorrow," are but the final movements in a narrative that suggests fraud and hopelessness from beginning to end. The opening paragraph, for example, quite appropriately begins with a reference to one of the most deceptive of all foods—croquettes—deceptive because the ingredients are disguised. The Corneliuses, a very "proper" middle class family, living in an illusory house outwardly appearing elegant but actually badly in need of repair, a house in which "they themselves look odd . . . with their worn and turned clothing and "altered way of life," sit to eat a dinner of "croquettes made of turnip greens" followed by a trifle that is "concocted out of those dessert powders" that the reader learns really taste like something else—soap (182).

Here we have a small example at the outset of how Mann uses a stylistic device called "parody of externals" to create irony, a subject that John G. Root discusses in an enlightening article on Mann's Style, but one which has never been successfully applied to an analysis of "Disorder and Early Sorrow." This brief study will attempt to explain how the *leitmotiv* of deception in this unusual tale is reinforced through the description of physical externals. We will find that in each character considered, except one, outer traits complement inner peculiarities. The one exception is the servant, Xaver, who has the ironic last name of Kleinsgutl, ironic because be is without doubt the only character in the story who is "his own man."

In contrast to Xaver, the other characters are poseurs, bearing more resemblance to puppets or mannequins than to real beings. The "big folks" (Bert and Ingrid), for instance, seem to lack integrity. They are much like the telephone that plays such a prominent part in their lives: expressionless, capable only of audible contact, an artificial sound device. Bert, the professor's seventeen year old son, having succumbed to Ivor Herzl's influence, "blackens the lower rim of his eyelids" and assumes the unnatural pose of a performer (184). Like Oscar Wilde's Dorian Gray, who is a creation of the artistic imagination of Lord Henry Wotton, Bert is Herzl's creation. From a distance, Bert is said to resemble Xaver, but there the resemblance ends; the doubles are inconsonant—Xaver is not a puppet. He toys with the idea of being engaged by a cinema director, but he is, as the Professor envisions, too much of a "good-for-nothing . . . with quite distinct traits of character of his own" ever to take the cinema dream seriously (205). He must be taken "as be is" (ibid.). Xaver does what he has the urge to do (he smokes thirty cigarettes a day, for instance); Bert, because he lacks "the means to compete with Xaver," or, for that matter, with anyone else, is forced to mimic others. Bert's deficiency manifests itself by the paternal envy his father experiences when comparing Bert's failures with the accomplishments of a number of male guests at the party. Bert's fraudulent, showy outward behavior mirrors his inner failure: "'poor Bert, who knows nothing and can do nothing . . . except playing the clown'" (204). His external appearance parodies his hollow, self-deception.

Ingrid, the Professor's older daughter, is also a markedly deceptive character whose entire life appears to have been comprised of sham and impersonation. She is said to know how to "wind masters, and even headmasters, round her finger" (182), and she is in school working for a certificate that she never plans to use. The performance that she and Bert put on in the bus, at the expense of the unhappy old gentleman sitting opposite them, and the delight she takes in ridiculing Max Hergesell's nasal drawl reflect a bizarre and sadistic inner quality. Both she and Bert foreshadow through their outward behavior the pose and affectation which will later distinguish the many painted figures who turn up for the party. (. . .)

The devastating irony that Mann achieves mainly through the parody of externals in this story reaches its culmination in the characterization of the Professor. The *leitmotiv* of deception, that pervades the story, ends with the lie that appears at the end of the narrative— the lie that the professor forces himself to believe: that tomorrow the glittering Hergesell will be, for Ellie, "a pale shadow" (216). The story, however, suggests otherwise. His prayers to heaven that Ellie will forget Hergesell and the festive world he symbolizes is the professor's final act of self-deception. She will not forget.

—Franklin E. Court, "Deception and the 'Parody of Externals' in Thomas Mann's 'Disorder and Early Sorrow.'" *Studies in Short Fiction* 12, no. 2 (Spring 1975): pp. 186–87, 188.

SIDNEY BOLKOSKY ON THE GOLDEN PAST

[Sidney Bolkosky is William E. Stirton Professor in the Social Sciences at the University of Michigan–Dearborn. His books include *Mighty Myth: A Modern Interpretation of Greek Myths for the Classroom* and *Harmony and Dissonance: Voices of Jewish Identity in Detroit*. His study of the story focuses on Professor Cornelius and his longing for Germany's golden past.]

"Disorder and Early Sorrow" is a "realistic" description of a day in the life of an upper middle-class family in the Munich of 1924. It has, however, deeper significance, suggesting an analysis of the time more pointed than any of Mann's previous aesthetic undertakings. He seems almost off his guard, somehow at ease, with a keen if relaxed eye for historical results. Written in 1925 at and about a time when the turbulent circumstances of people's lives were indisputably attributable to such a monumental political event as World War I, the narrative makes a political statement and embodies Mann's evolving feelings about life in the Weimar Republic and the future of Germany.

The war had brought Germans impoverishment, austerity, debt, a collection of revolutions and *Putsch*, unbelievable inflation, malaise, cynicism, imbalance, loss of values, and a rejection of history. Both the nation and families were wracked by generational conflict and rebellion. Instead of *Kultur*, "dedication to a basic order of things and its lasting values," there was disorder, which Mann addressed here, from its midst, in every conceivable aspect. In "Disorder and Early Sorrow" he satirized what one critic has dubbed his "seismographic neutrality" through a poignant self-accusation, and he expressed moral, historical, social, and political opinions—unequivocally. (. . .)

In the center of the activity, a bit confused and frazzled by the commotion, a bit absent-minded, is Professor Abel Cornelius. His name suits him: "Cornelius" evokes a portrait of a classical and patriotic outlook and "Abel," the obedient servant of authority, formal, precise and faithful—but doomed. He is the *"geistiger Mensch,"* akin in some respects to Aschenbach, but more to Mann himself. As historian, he is faithful to the past, obsessed with time, watching clocks and calendars, losing track of the days, trying to hold time back and to become history. He is old Germany: the historian as state bureaucrat, pedantic civil servant, teacher and authority figure who, before World War I, was conformist, unquestioning, and, most importantly, apolitical. Because of his love for the past, for the "timeless," the "eternal," and "infinity," he hates the revolution. But as an apolitical man by scholarly principle and commitment, he does not confront it actively. Abel has made compromises: he has shaved his pointed beard (probably reminiscent of the Kaiser), for example, and silently tolerated the laziness and near-insolence of the servants and children.

When the present confronts him, Cornelius "withdraws to his study." Mann does not have him "go," "retire," or "move," but "withdraw" (*Zurückziehen*), a word that increasingly implies retreat. And there he reads. Is reading perhaps an escape from disorder? A way to combat it? Words seem to control past events in the historian's "art," to order them clearly and to define and explain rationally the flow of history. Unchanging words provide unchanging significance and meaning for him, while perfectly ordered syntax provides perfectly ordered history; both disappear in the world of the party. What attracts the historian, Abel thinks, is the certainty and order of the past—certain, even immortal, because it is dead "and death is the root of all godliness and abiding significance." Such pious Hegelian ruminations sound not profound, but foolish, irrelevant, almost quaint in the historical context of this story. Dutiful Abel withdraws to his inner sanctum and escapes the living present and its hostile insecurities by reading of "genuine history," the dead past. The washbasin, broken for two years, remains unfixed, the quest for eggs not his worry, the myriad of minor and major crises remote from him. And the language of the young remains unintelligible to him, alienating him from his children, from the party, from real life and action.

Professor Cornelius is simultaneously a realistic figure and a rich literary symbol of a way of life that was fast fading from existence in 1924. He encapsulates more than the "preoccupation with death of a typical bourgeois of the pre-war period" in Lukács' limiting description of him." Life in his study is the life of the mind, replete with words separated from action and reality. He reads backwards in time: first of England in the seventeenth century, the origin of the English public debt; then of Spain's enormous debt at the close of the sixteenth century. Here is food for a lecture comparing the prosperity of England despite its debt with the catastrophic failure of Spain under similar circumstances. A wealth of material rests in the English and French texts from which the professor will form an ethical and psychological analysis. All this provides a means of discussing his specialty, Philip II of Spain and the Counter-Reformation.

(Cornelius has already written a monograph on the subject.) In his self-contained refuge, Abel makes no connection whatsoever between these historical crises and that of Germany in 1924, between the end of Spain's Empire and the collapse of Germany's in wars against England. His failure to do so is breathtaking in its blindness. This boundary between mind and matter, this divorce from reality testifies to a fatal flaw in those of Abel's class, profession, and ethos. And Mann does not justify it, sympathize with it, or pity it. We feel the pathos of Abel's situation, but no sympathy for his separation; no meditative, artistic excuses for disengagement insinuate themselves.

—Sidney Bolkosky, "Thomas Mann's 'Disorder and Early Sorrow':
The Writer as Social Critic." Contemporary Literature 22, no. 2
(Spring 1981): pp. 221, 224–25.

ESTHER H. LESÉR ON ORDER AND DISORDER

[Esther H. Lesér is Professor Emeritus of Germanic, Romance, and Comparative Philology at the University of North Dakota and is author of *Thomas Mann's Short Fiction: An Intellectual Biography*. The following extract, taken from that book, illustrates the kinds of "disorder" that threaten the stability of the Cornelius family.]

Professor Cornelius, the father and narrator, embodies the theme, as he responds to the disruption and to the warmth of his heart, shown principally with his small daughter Lorchen. The "big folk's" party catalyzes the story in its three parts: the introduction; the party itself, where the younger generation contrasts the professor's feelings; and the representation of "disorder" as the source of little Lorchen's overwhelming experience. The characters' expressions are readily discernible in their dialogue. It reveals, for example, the obvious good nature with which the parents meet their disconcerting lack of means, the mother's worries, her fatigue and her inability to get away for a rest—all are expressed with a light ironic fatalism.

The preparation for the party, in the slangy unconventional fashion of Ingrid and Bert, is a little suspect to the adults, but it seems to them attractive, even desirable. "The *bürgerlich* old ones have a harder time" (EHL) (*GW*, 8: 621; see also *STD*, 503). The "*Bürger*" concept here has nothing to do with the "*Künstler*" seen in earlier short stories, especially "Tonio Kröger." Also the concept of the *Bürger* has another meaning, and it is contrasted in a peculiar fashion with the young ones' ways, appearing nostalgic, old-fashioned, out of the main stream of things, but cultured and in a way respected. Nevertheless the young people show all the signs of respect to their hosts' parents; they are friendly and accept the presence of the "little ones" with good nature and without ceremony. The professor is almost shocked at these positive qualities.

The open-mindedness that helped Mann over the *Betrachtungen* also appears in this story's acknowledgment of the youngsters' basic decency. They are surmounting the paradoxes of a world gone mad, without the second thoughts or the regrets of the older generation. The evil "Disorder" of this world malignantly affects the people born into it, as Thomas Mann demonstrates through the distortions and paradoxical clashes of all these young people, culminating in Lorchen's outburst, a symptom of the disruption of the times. Mann had already used the unusual expression "historical man" in the *Betrachtungen*, and he defined it clearly in this short story: "... professors of history do not love history when it happens, only when it already has happened; . . . they hate the upheaval of the present because they conceive it as lawless, lacking continuity, fresh, in one word, 'unhistorical' and . . . their hearts belong to the historical part" (EHL) (see also *STD*, 506; *GW*, 8: 626–27). Mann's use of "historical" demonstrates the disengaged *Weltanschauung* of the "unpolitical." The professor Cornelius's goatee resembles Heinrich Mann's, and his "long" nose and small mouth resemble those of both father and his son. Heinrich's pro-French, anti-German attitude had changed, just as Thomas Mann had overcome his own emotional conservatism with the *Betrachtungen*, and both had been disillusioned by the partisan profanity of postwar politics. Contributing wittily to the "disorder," Mann knowingly mingled their personal qualities, both physical and *geistig*, in Professor Cornelius.

The "disorder" of the world has been forced upon the professor, and he is caught between his own tendency to timeless historical "order" and the shocking "disorder" all around him. He is no longer the respected master of his house, but a questor, spurred by the thirst for discovery and gravely anxious about the unknown. This semiautobiographical figure candidly expresses the *Künstler*-questor's simultaneous fear of and longing for the world that Thomas Mann himself felt. This mood, an ironic antithesis of the great questor heroes of cultural history, was for him a profound human experience. The solemn grandeur of the *nunc stans*, as the professor conceives the historical past, illustrates all of man's existence.

The connotations of "disorder" as pertinent to the concepts of culture, history, and the unpolitical illuminate Professor Cornelius's conceptual problems. In a "culture," a group of people accept a common *geistig* way as an "order" they willingly accept; "order" is thus synonymous with "culture." Within this formal and traditional frame the individual finds and gains self-expression, which "order" keeps from infringing on others. In their golden ages, nations possess this order or cultural unity, but after such periods equilibrium loses appeal and becomes rigid, often phasing into hypocrisy and corruption. In such an era, supposed claims for free expression are merely fresh attempts to undermine the aging cultural order, eventually rusting out the traditional mechanism that inertia keeps going. "Disorder" ranges from "mutiny" to "vital new spirit;" it may cause a tragic collapse, or it may begin new trends that could develop another golden age of "order." The cycles of recurring cultural orders regulate general mores and styles of language, allowing the individual freedom of expression without limiting others. Achieving such balance, however, is difficult without intellectual and spiritual excellence, free from pragmatic corruption and from the intellectualizing of *geistig* values, which Professor Cornelius called "unhistory" and Thomas Mann considered the spirit of "Western civilization." "Order" or "disorder" is then a *geistig* and artistic phenomenon rather than a symptom of civilization, which tends toward rationalism and pragmatism. The professor's concept of the "historical" parallels the "unpolitical," synonymous with "order," and he therefore opposes the "disorder" of economic, behavioral, and cultural structures that allow blind impulse and instinct to rule.

—Esther H. Lesér, *Thomas Mann's Short Fiction: An Intellectual Biography*, ed. Mitzi Brunsdale (Rutherford, N.J.: Fairleigh Dickinson University Press, 1989): pp. 189–90.

[Anthony Heilbut has taught at New York University and Hunter College. He is author the acclaimed biography *Thomas Mann: Eros and Literature* and *Exiled in Paradise: German Refugee Artists and Intellectuals in America*. He is also a regular contributor to the *New York Times Book Review*. His biographical reading identifies the story as the first by Mann to present a parent's point of view.]

The professor himself is a pretty queer fellow. Perhaps no writer before Mann had so captured the obsessive nature of parental love. Cornelius adores Lorchen as intensely as Aschenbach loves Tadzio. His feelings are not quite without calculation. He has been "preparing for it . . . been prepared for it." A sense of duty and obligation have finally paid off: as Mann wrote, Elisabeth was the first child he spontaneously loved. His "conservative instinct" finds an eternal image in "father love and a little child on its mother's breast." But this affirmation of "family values" is a rear-guard strategy. "There is something ulterior about it, in the nature of it; that something is hostility, hostility against the history of today, which is still in the making and thus not history at all, in behalf of the genuine history that has already happened—that is to say, death."

We remember that this story is composed in the present tense, unlike *The Magic Mountain*, with its counterpoint of historically ripened moments. Sure enough, Mann observes that Cornelius's devotion has "something to do with death, it clings to death as against life, and that is neither right nor beautiful—in a sense." Paternal love becomes a political statement! In Cornelius's ideology, the nuclear family symbolizes death; and the post-heterosexual choreography, its living—and terrifying—alternative.

The youngsters jabber away while Cornelius retires in gloom. Anything can set him off. The cigarette smoke becomes "particularly poignant to those whose youth—like the professor's own—has been oversensitive." (There may be an echo of Mann's early tales of tobacco-induced highs.) He chooses Philip II because he exemplifies "things steeped in melancholy and penetratingly just." Therefore, while "it behooves one to display the scientific spirit, to exhibit the principles of enlightenment," simply not to offend anyone's political sensibility, he can't quite manage this epistemological pluralism (a reflection of the "Neue Sachlichkeit"—New Objectivity—that supposedly characterized the 1920s). Justice has a "secret affinity with the lost cause," even if his children tell him that "taking sides is unhistoric now."

Only one of the young guests shares his feelings. The actor Herzl (Gründgens?) is a "revolutionary artist" with a bad conscience. He wears rouge but is "exaggeratedly polite" to "mitigate its effect." Cornelius wonders, "How can a melancholy man rouge?" Coming from a Mann brother, Heinrich or Thomas, this qualifies as a rhetorical question.

The essayistic musings on history are interrupted by word that Lorchen has become hysterical. But Max comes to the rescue; the idea is Xaver's. He kisses Lorchen's forehead, begs her not to dream of him—"not at your age"—and leaves her to sleep away her troubles. The professor's response is ambivalent. In the great tradition of Tonio Kröger, he feels "thankfulness, embarrassment and hatred." Attraction, too, we can guess.

The happy ending self-destructs. Cornelius thinks of a tale in which a dying child asks to see a clown "he had once, with unforgettable ecstasy, beheld in a circus." The clown appears, and the child dies contented; even Cornelius finds this analogy morbid. But he's not only grieving for his child. Mann/Cornelius brings his own years of rejection to the "big folks'" dance. His own chance had passed, had he ever possessed the will to grab it, and now the child of his heart would live again the Mannian cycle of unrequited love.

Even without this highly biographical reading, "Early Sorrow" marks a transition in Mann's career, quite literally from offspring to parent. In his earlier works the sons had caught out the fathers—whether it was Hanno seeing through his father's disguise, or Felix Krull reporting on the "poison" his father bottled as wine—and helped to bury them. Likewise, sexual precocity was experienced by the youthful subjects, even that delayed adolescent Hans Castorp. But starting with this story, Mann's focus switches. Now it's the father who sees desire manifest itself, virtually in the cradle.

—Anthony Heilbut, *Thomas Mann: Eros and Literature*, (New York: Knopf, 1996): pp. 448–49.

[David Turner is Senior Lecturer in German at the University of Hull in England and is author of *Moral Values and the Human Zoo: The Novellen of Stefan Zweig*. Here he argues for the limited perspective of the narrator, who is influenced by the central character's values as well as his point of view.]

Even for the reader of *Unordnung und frühes Leid* who is unaware of any autobiographical connections there is one especially powerful and pervasive feature of narrative presentation which, alone and unqualified, would encourage an unduly sympathetic understanding: the story is told almost entirely from Cornelius's point of view. The author has not, it is true, adopted that first-person voice which can so easily seduce the unwary in *Mario und der Zauberer*, but his third-person narrator appears to have aligned himself so thoroughly with the professor's perspective that the danger is potentially no less great.

At the simplest level it is a matter of how, with one or two insignificant or doubtful exceptions, the narrator describes only what lies within Cornelius's immediate or remembered experience. When during the course of the single day recorded in the story the professor comes downstairs after taking a short nap, the festivities organised by his older children are described as he gradually becomes aware of them; when he retreats to his study for a time, the young people's dancing to their modern music is presented not directly but as heard by him through the wall; when he goes out for a walk, the narrator follows him and his reflections, turning his back on the party that is continuing indoors. Even when, near the beginning of the story, the narrator temporarily abandons Cornelius to recount some of the pretences and practical jokes of Bert and Ingrid, of which their father is unaware, he introduces the professor's perspective by proxy, in the protests of an elderly gentleman with academic pretensions, who objects to their public discussion of such ostensibly improper behaviour (623).

Thomas Mann's narrator not only limits himself almost entirely to what lies within the range of Cornelius's perception; he also tends to adopt the values of his central character. It is a feature of the narrative voice of *Unordnung und frühes Leid* that, although there are passages where it describes Cornelius from the outside and with apparent neutrality and there are other passages where it assumes his mask in the form of narrated or even interior monologue, for most of the time it occupies shifting ground between the two, assimilating the vocabulary and values of Professor Cornelius to varying degrees and in such a way that the stance may alter within a single sentence or the reader may be unable to determine with any certainty whether the information offered represents the view of the narrator, that of the professor, or that of some amalgam of the two.

Consider the following extract, describing some of the domestic staff in the Cornelius household, starting with one of two sisters who occupy their present position only because they have come down in the world. (. . .)

At various points the passage moves beyond the terms of a factual report, and offers a series of personal judgements on the two figures presented ('eine gefallene Königin'; 'ein ausgemachter Taugenichts und Windbeutel'; 'ein Kind und Früchtchen der gelösten Zeit . . . ein Revolutionsdiener, ein sympathischer Bolschewist'). But it is impossible to be sure whether they represent the views of the narrator, the views of Cornelius or of both equally. All one can say for certain is that they do not differ from the views of Cornelius implied elsewhere in the story and that they are not disowned by the narrator either. At other points the passage implies the stance of an eyewitness who both observes and responds emotionally to what he has observed ('eine Qual . . . mit anzusehen'; 'Offensichtlich ..., und das entwaffnet und stimmt zum Verzicht'). In these instances the reader is less likely to identify the perspective with that of the narrator, since the clearest evidence of the reported 'Qual' is the tears of the professor's younger children, which have presumably served to reinforce their father's reaction, while the one who is disarmed and persuaded to renounce is evidently the professor himself (and perhaps his wife). The perspective is undoubtedly one in which Cornelius shares; it is also one from which the narrator nevertheless does not seek to distance himself. (. . .)

In short, what is likely to remain the reader's strongest impression on reading *Unordnung und frühes Leid* and what could be illustrated by many other more extended passages is that the narrative perspective seems largely to embrace that of the central character, even though to an extent which does not remain static and is not always clearly definable.

—David Turner, "Balancing the Account: Thomas Mann's *Unordnung und frühes Leid." German Life and Letters* 12, no. 1 (January 1999): pp. 44–46, 47.

Tonio Kröger

As with *Buddenbooks* and many of Mann's subsequent works, *Tonio Kröger* draws heavily on the author's experiences. Like Mann, the title character of this novella written in 1903 is deeply conscious of his mixed background and his longing for bourgeois life. The story's two-part structure, presenting Tonio Kröger's struggles as a child and then as an adult, offers an insightful perspective on the development of this compelling individual.

The story opens on a winter afternoon as Tonio is waiting by the school gates for Hans Hansen, a blond, blue-eyed schoolmate whom he plans to walk home with. When his friend finally arrives Tonio distressingly realizes that Hans has forgotten their plans. Hans, however, manages to lift Tonio's spirits with his charm. After they part ways, Tonio observes that he loves Hans more than the boy loves him, and that his inferior position will always be a source of pain.

Tonio is fond of his friend for all the things that he is not. Hans is popular and athletic, while he is a loner and enjoys poetry. He has tried to interest Hans in reading poetry, but he acknowledges that his friend's interest is only superficial at best. Tonio finds no encouragement for his artistic interests at school, where the recent discovery of his notebook of poems has given him the reputation of a shiftless dreamer. After receiving bad reports from his schoolteachers, Tonio's father scolds him, which the sensitive boy takes to heart. Tonio's mother is more forgiving about the reports, but as a foreigner "from some place far down on the map," her opinion is not nearly as important to him as his father's.

Tonio's infatuation for Hans passes with his sudden interest in Inge Holm, a blond, perpetually cheerful girl from his dance class. Like Hans, Inge is very typical, which for Tonio provides for much of her charm. During a quadrille in which Tonio makes a clumsy mistake, the ballet instructor Herr Knaak humiliates the boy in front of everyone. The scene lingers in Tonio's memory long afterwards because he knows that Inge laughed at him along with the other children. Magdalena Vermehren, a classmate of Tonio's who also loves poetry, likes him, but he shows no interest for a kindred spirit. He only longs for Inge, though he acknowledges that nothing—not even poetry—can win her favor. He also realizes that only people like Inge, who have no need for serious literature, can find happiness. The discovery does not persuade him to forsake his love of poetry, but it does sustain his longing for the bourgeois life in his years to come as a writer.

During the period while Tonio is deciding on a career, his father's mother, the matron of the family's grain business, dies. Soon after, Tonio's father dies and the Kröger mansion goes up for sale. As a result of the turn of events, Tonio is impelled to leave home and follow what he believes is his destiny as a writer. He moves to southern Europe to find inspiration, but before he finds any success, he succumbs to "adventures of the flesh," followed by periods of deep remorse. For some time he wavers between the extremes of the intellectual and the sensual life.

Eventually he becomes an established author and moves north to Munich, where his erratic behavior subsides and he finds friends of a similar temperament. One day he becomes unsatisfied with his current project and unloads his worries on Lisabeta Ivaanovna, a painter and supportive friend. He regrets to have learned that a writer must be emotionless if he wants to preserve his detached view of human nature. He also complains that the knowledge he has acquired through his craft serves no practical purpose, and he pities any bourgeois individual who aspires to poetry. Literature, he concludes, is not a calling but a curse, and a writer must sacrifice nearly everything for the glory he attains. Lisabeta responds to his grumbling by simply calling him a "bourgeois on the wrong path." Tonio apparently accepts her assessment wholeheartedly, because he thanks her and abruptly leaves the room.

Several months later, Tonio plans a trip north to Denmark. Along the way he passes through his hometown, which he has not seen for 13 years. As he walks through the old streets, he is beset with foggy memories and the fear that he will stumble upon someone from his past. He thinks of his father, and though he has been dead for years, his discouraging comments echo in Tonio's mind. He finally reaches his old home, which to his surprise has become a public library. While passing through the library rooms, he finds that his old bedroom has been filled with books, perhaps a symbolic recognition of his calling as a writer. When he looks outside the window and spots an old walnut tree, one of the few things that have not disappeared, he becomes overwhelmed with nostalgia

After deciding that he has seen enough, he returns to the hotel and prepares to leave. His departure is delayed when the hotel owner, Herr Seehaase, asks to speak with him. Accompanying Herr Seehaase is a policeman, clearly suspicious of Tonio, who asks to see his papers. Tonio states that he has none, after which the incited policeman accuses Tonio of being someone who is charged with fraud. Herr Seehaase steps in and asks Tonio if he can provide any form of identity, whereupon he produces his galley proofs. When the two men see Tonio's name on the proofs, and that he is a published author, the investigation ends, as does Tonio's unsettling visit to his hometown.

Once aboard the ship to Copenhagen, Tonio becomes vexed when he remembers the confrontation back at the hotel, but he soon turns his attention to the boat as it prepares to embark. That evening a merchant from Hamburg joins Tonio on the deck and tries to poetically describe the night stars. Unimpressed, Tonio recalls his pity for the bourgeois and their vain attempts at artistic expression. When he arrives to the bustling city of Copenhagen, Tonio sees scores of blond and blue-eyed people, who make him feel self-conscious once again. He decides to move on to nearby Helsingör, and soon arrives at a small seaside hotel for an extended stay.

For several days Tonio enjoys his peaceful stay, despite the gray, stormy weather he encounters. On a morning when the sun finally appears, several buses full of guests arrive at the hotel. He learns from another guest that the newly arrived are preparing for a ball later that night. Then he spots Hans Hansen and Inge Holm passing through the room together. While he has not seen or thought of either individual in years, they remain for him perfect specimens of purity and simplicity. He anxiously waits for the ball later that evening, at which he will try to work up the courage to approach Hans and Inge.

When the time of the ball arrives, Tonio decides to watch from behind a glass door on the veranda. As he observes Inge and Hans across the room, he pines for their normal and innocent life. He also notices a pale, homely girl with no dancing partner, whom he assumes is Hans's sister. The dancers begin to notice Tonio, and the pale girl, peers invitingly at him. As he did years before with

Magdalena Vermehren, Tonio ignores the girl and keeps his attention on Inge and Hans. He thinks of something to say, but halts before approaching them, convincing himself that they would want nothing to do with him.

The dancers become more animated and at one point gather for a quadrille. Tonio's face reddens as the scene calls up his memories of his blunder years before. He remains apart from the dancers, haunted by the memory of Inge laughing at him. The sad truth occurs to Tonio that no artistic achievement of his could keep someone like Inge from ever laughing at him, even now. Two dancers begin to lose control and a girl falls directly in front of Tonio. He helps her to her feet, informs her that she probably should not dance anymore, and abruptly leaves the ballroom.

Back in his hotel room, Tonio begins to sob. He longs to be part of the "lulling, trivial waltz-rhythm" he can still softly hear in the ballroom below the floor. However, his sorrow is also mixed with a sense of contentment. He is comforted by the thought that things are as they should be—a feeling he has experienced before, but never so deeply and with such insight. He decides to articulate his thoughts in a letter to Lisabeta, in which he declares that being a "bourgeois on the wrong path," as she called him, is exactly what inspires his love for life. He refuses to give up his love for the bourgeois life because he feels that it is a vital part of him, and it is the source of his writing's true value. "For if anything is capable of making a poet of a literary man," he concludes, "it is my *bourgeois* love of the human, the living and usual."

Tonio Kröger

Tonio Kröger is the sensitive, highly contemplative writer and hero of the novella. His mixed heritage endows him with an artist's soul and bourgeois sentiments, and he realizes that his unrequited love for the bourgeois life is the source of his long-lasting sorrow, as well as his ultimate value as a poet.

Consul Kröger is Tonio's practical father, always described as having a wild flower in his buttonhole. Years after Consul Kröger's death, Tonio still fears his contempt for his idle ways.

Consuelo Kröger is Tonio's fiery mother from southern Europe who passes on to him his love for art. Although she is more forgiving about Tonio's poor school reports, he does not heed her opinion as much as his father's.

Hans Hansen is Tonio's athletic and popular boyhood friend who never returns Tonio's affections. He reappears years later as the self-assured husband of Ingle Holm at the hotel where Tonio stays.

Inge Holm is the blond, cheerful girl who is the object of Tonio's longing following his obsession with Hans. To Tonio's dismay, she laughs at him when he embarrasses himself at their dance lesson.

François Knaak is the illustrious and pompous ballet instructor who humiliates Tonio when he blunders during a quadrille.

Magdalena Vermehren, Tonio's plain-looking classmate, is the only one to show interest in his poetry.

Lisabeta Ivanovna is Tonio's painter friend during his years as a successful writer in Munich. She listens patiently to his lengthy complaint about his difficulties as a writer, then concludes that he is a "bourgeois on the wrong path."

Herr Seehaase is the manager of the hotel where Tonio stays during his return visit to his hometown. He mediates between Tonio and Officer Petersen when Tonio is interrogated as a criminal suspect.

Officer Petersen is the suspicious investigator who accuses Tonio of being a fraud. He ends his questioning when Tonio proves his identity as a successful author.

CRITICAL VIEWS ON

Tonio Kröger

Elizabeth M. Wilkinson on the Alienation of the Artist

[Elizabeth M. Wilkinson was Professor of German at University College London. She edited *On the Aesthetic Education of Man, in a Series of Letters* by Friedrich Schiller, and wrote *Johann Elias Schlegel: A German Pioneer in Aesthetics* and *Goethe's Conception of Form*. Her introduction to an early edition of the novella focuses on the alienation that Tonio Kröger must endure as an artist.]

In this story Thomas Mann dwells mainly on the pain which awareness brings, on the separating effect of this kind of knowledge. Its compensations are ignored. Yet they are very real, as Tonio must ultimately have known. The joy it brings outweighs the pain. And even though awareness may make the pangs of suffering sharper, it yet removes from it the destructive quality of blind sorrow. To be so involved that we can see nothing beyond ourselves, to be so completely sufferer that light is shut out, and we grope along in the darkness of almost animal pain, is a deadening experience. "Dumpfheit" Goethe called such blind living, and preferred "ewig klingende Existenz," whether it brought him joy or sorrow.

This awareness, the power of being absorbed in something beyond oneself, of responding to the essential quality of a thing or event, the artist shares with others. But in him the mood is more intense and more permanent. The differentiation within the self is such that he more continuously perceives meanings which are hidden when we are absorbed in our own affairs. Of him it is especially true that "there is one man in us who acts and one who watches." Thomas Mann holds fast for us the very moment when this watching trembles on the brink of becoming literature, the transition from awareness to the communication of it through the medium of words. We can distinguish four phases in Tonio's love for Hans; not in time, for they may have happened in one single illumination, but in quality and depth of experience. First he loved Hans and suffered much on his account. That is a purely personal experience expressed in particular terms. Then he was so organized that he received such experiences consciously and recognized the hard fact that he who loves more must suffer more. That is a general human experience expressed in universal terms. But now—and this is the transition from "watching" to "shaping"—"er schrieb sie innerlich auf", that is, the experience became formed, a kind of blue-print of a poem. Finally we get the hall-mark of the artist, the pleasure in the experience, with all its bitter knowledge, for its own sake, without any thought of its practical value for his living: "er hatte gewissermaßen an diesen Erfahrungen seine Freude, ohne sich freilich für seine Person danach zu richten und praktischen Nutzen daraus zu ziehen."

Much of Tonio's delight in his beloved "Springbrunnen, Walnußbaum, seine Geige und in der Ferne das Meer, die Ostsee," is due to the music of their names, "Namen, die mit guter Wirkung in Versen zu verwenden sind." It is the delight the poet takes in calling "the bright, unshadowed things he sees by name." When Lisaweta speaks of the "redeeming power of the word," she surely means that through his medium the artist's insight becomes manifestly fruitful. But again Tonio chooses to ignore the rewards and to dwell rather on the toll which the artist must pay for having surrendered to the power of his medium, a toll paid in sterility and isolation. Even as early as his love for Inge, Tonio realized that he must be in some sense remote from an experience in order to be able to "form" it into literature, remote, not in space or time, but attitude. Later his joy in the word and the need for "distance" took such possession of him that he became merely an onlooker of himself and others. The roots of such an artist's loneliness lie deeper than is normally supposed. The restlessness which chafes at domesticity, the need to conserve his energy, these are only the more superficial aspects of the problem. His inner loneliness springs rather from his deep sense of failure as a human being. At some point in an experience words become more exciting to him than the experience itself. Even in an intimate relationship he fears he may be side-tracked by his artist's eye, his urge to form may suddenly "see" it, crying out to be shaped by his hand into a work of art, so that he fails as a human being.

—Elizabeth M. Wilkinson, Introduction to *Tonio Kröger,* (Oxford: Basil Blackwell, 1944): pp. xxix–xxxi.

[Kenneth G. Wilson was Fulbright Professor at the University of Bergen in Norway and Professor of English at the University of Connecticut–Storrs, and has written a number of reference books, including the *Columbia Guide to Standard American English*. Here he concentrates on the symbolism of dance in two crucial scenes of the novella.

THE OLD, honored metaphor of life as dance is a basis of both structure and theme in Thomas Mann's *Tonio Kröger*. The dance often serves literature as a figure in little of man's social existence; man and woman are partners as they express their feelings through a pouring-out of physical and emotional energies according to a rhythmic pattern. Mann is a civilized author and is writing of Tonio, a civilized poet; he uses as symbol the quadrille, a civilized dance of couples, a "society" square dance. The quadrille, with its five parts, is a particularly sophisticated dance form; the patterns are highly complex, rigidly conventional, and extremely formal, although the pace and the level of emotional and physical expression are often enthusiastic and sometimes even boisterous. In essence the dance is a seeking of partners; in the quadrille, the social patterns are strictly ordered: boy meets girl, loses and finds her again and again in the intricate patterns, and finally recovers her just as the dance ends. All physical and emotional expression, however spirited, is rigorously controlled. The dancers may not proceed according to will or caprice or inspiration, but must be skilled in following the maze of the pattern. They must train their bodies to perform a series of mechanical reflexes, and they must have an instinctive awareness of their relationship to the pattern, because there are so many dancers that one misstep by an awkward individual will destroy the whole ordered pattern of the dance. The implications of the dance as metaphor are both personal and social, and the thread of the dance can be broken both by those who cannot master the skills and so fall down in the dance, and by those who cannot close their minds to everything but their part in the dance, and so fail to concentrate themselves into a simple state of emotional and physical expression.

In *Tonio Kröger* the dance as symbolic act is employed structurally only in the first, second, and last episodes; thematically, its use is more widespread, but suggestive rather than rigid. Once it has been thoroughly established as a metaphor it often serves simply as a kind of leitmotiv, several of which Mann employs profusely throughout the story? There are many such formulas which serve as figures for ideas or complexes of feeling, if one considers change and development and structural integration necessary to the symbol. The leitmotiv in *Tonio Kröger*, as distinct from the fully developed symbol, is a constant which, while it may symbolize roughly, stands for an unarticulated and undifferentiated complex of idea and feeling. It serves exactly as does a Wagnerian leitmotiv, as an announcement or reminder of matters which cannot be stated fully. For example: Tonio's mother is dark, southern, fiery, and somehow irresponsible; his father is tall, fastidious, silent, and somehow northern. But the *matter* behind these phrases and words is never made more explicit; the diction remains the only concretion, and merely suggests idea. The story is not a study of heredity, except in the broadest sense. Tonio is like both his parents, but they are so deliberately oversimplified in their respective southernness and northernness that even the compass qualities are merely suggestive and relative. They recur several times in the story, but without development or change; they are leitmotivs, consciously formulated and petrified references, which are then repeated to evoke in the reader a constant recognition whenever they occur. Unquestionably, all these leitmotivs invite predominantly emotional rather than intellectual grasp by the reader. The dance and the dancer are often thematically employed like leitmotivs, but structurally they serve as symbols, for they involve change and development, and they invite both intellectual and emotional understanding in the reader. The structural use of the dance is simple: the dancers seek love, and the final position is a claiming of partners. Tonio as would-be dancer begins with Hans Hansen, fails to win him, turns to Ingeborg, fails again, and then seeks Lisabeta, though not as a partner in the usual sense of the dance; with Lisabeta and throughout the remainder of the story he is simply trying to find a way into the dance; the dance goes on without him. After his failure to gain recognition in his home town, he goes back to the blue-eyed, blond-haired dancers, only to withdraw in the end while the dance continues without him. He can hear the music and laughter and excitement of the dance, but he must remain apart. He can only watch, or stare at himself in shuttered windows, or stand outside the hall; in the end he goes away to dance alone to another rhythm, "the cruel and perilous sword-dance of art" (130). He can never dance the quadrille. All his attempts are unfinished.

—Kenneth G. Wilson, "The Dance as Symbol and Leitmotiv in Thomas Mann's *Tonio Kröger.*" *Germanic Review* 29, no. 4 (December 1954): pp. 282–83.

GEORG LUKÁCS ON THE BOURGEOIS LIFE

[Georg Lukács (1885–1971), a Hungarian philosopher and literary historian, was a peer of Mann's as well as an eminent critic. Many of his writings, such as *The Theory of the Novel* (1920) and *History and Class Consciousness* (1923), have had a great influence on Marxist criticism. In the following extract, taken from a collection of essays on Mann, he discusses the consequences of Tonio Kröger's decision to leave his bourgeois life behind.]

The Russian painter, Lisaveta Ivanovna, calls her friend Tonio Kröger a 'bourgeois run astray'. And Tonio himself sees clearly on the one hand that a real art (a real culture and morality) could only be achieved in his day by taking the path he had chosen. On the other hand he loves life and rates it higher than an art forced to stand aside from life. His description of life is very bourgeois: 'Don't think of Caesar Borgia or any drunken philosophy that has him for a standard bearer. He is nothing to me, your Caesar Borgia. I have no opinion of him, and I shall never comprehend how one can honour the extraordinary and daemonic as an ideal. No, life as the eternal antimony of mind and art does not represent itself to us as a vision of savage greatness and ruthless beauty; we who are set apart and different do not conceive it as, like us, unusual; it is the normal, respectable, and admirable that is the kingdom of our longing; life, in all its seductive banality!' We seem once more to have reached our goal. It is ordinary people like Hans Hansen and Ingeborg Holm who constitute bourgeois life. They do—in the dreams of Tonio and his kind. But if this discovery was anything more than a lyrical irony,

Thomas Mann would have had to give up all idea of a bourgeois culture. For the Hans Hansens and Ingeborg Holms have no more relevance to the cultural development of the German middle class from Goethe to Thomas Mann than the Hagenströms or the Klöterjahns, though they are considerably more attractive to look at, which fits them better as the objects of a dream. But even the most sincere of dreams is deceptive. In Mann's Fiorenza the dying Lorenzo di Medici says to Savonarola, 'Whither the longing urges, there one is not, that one is not—you know? And yet man likes to confuse himself with his longing.'

So it would seem after all that the 'bourgeois run astray', Tonio Kröger, Thomas Buddenbrook's soul-mate become writer, and the genuine bourgeois with his code of 'composure', embody the true ethic of the new bourgeoisie.

—Georg Lukács, *Essays on Thomas Mann*, trans. Stanley Mitchell (New York: Grosset & Dunlap, 1964): pp. 23–24.

LIDA KIRCHBERGER ON THE NOVELLA'S SOURCES

[Lida Kirchberger is Professor Emeritus of German at University of Wisconsin–Madison and author of *Franz Kafka's Use of Law in Fiction*. Her study of the novella focuses on two sources: Johann Wolfgang von Goethe's *The Sorrows of Young Werther* and Theodor Storm's *Immensee*.]

Beginning with the text of the Novelle itself, Thomas Mann has disclosed in many places the sources of inspiration for *Tonio Kröger*. Allusions to works such as Hamlet, Schiller's *Don Carlos*, or Wagner's *Tristan und Isolde* probably have little to do with its origins, but the tribute to Turgenjew and Storm implied in the gentleman "mit der Feldblume im Knopfloch" comes closer. Storm's part is also suggested in the line, "Ich möchte schlafen, aber du mußt tanzen," quoted during each of the two dance scenes. It is in the first of these that Tonio wonders why he is not at home reading *Immensee*, while his growing isolation is shown by contrast with the happy laughter of his dancing friends, people who do not read *Immensee* and never try to do anything like it themselves (*VIII*, p. 296).

Thomas Mann's belated discovery in *Betrachtungen eines Unpolitischen* that his Tonio is a brother of Schlemihl, Undine, and Heiling the Dutchman is not particularly relevant (*XII*, 92). More interesting is the statement a few pages later where *Tonio Kröger* is characterized as "ins Modern-Problematische fortgewandelter *Immensee*," as "eine Synthese aus Intellecktualismus und Stimmung, aus Nietzsche und Storm" (*XII*, 106). Scholars have not failed to note the analogy, though they have stopped short of a closer investigation of its implications, hardly surprising when in fact not Storm, but Goethe, must be placed first among poets on whom Thomas Mann relied both consciously and unconsciously for the composition of *Tonio Kröger*. In a number of letters Thomas Mann warns recipients not to look for his own person in the figure of Tonio Kröger, at the same time referring them to *Die Leiden des jungen Werthers*. (. . .)

If it were possible to note at length all the many aspects under which *Werther* and *Immensee* can be seen as contributory to *Tonio Kröger*, the sixth chapter might be a good place to start since here, at the beginning of the second part of the Novelle, Tonio Kröger, like Werther early in the second book, makes a pilgrimage to the birthplace he had left after the death of his father. The return home cannot but involve the heart, and with the words, "wie damals, als Tonio Kröger, nichts als Spott im Herzen, von hier gefahren war" (*VIII*, 307), the sixth chapter begins by recalling chapter three, where Tonio's heart had been pronounced dead. Before long Tonio is listening to the anxious throb of his heart (*VIII*, 310), and once more his heart pounds with anxiety (*VIII*, 311), as if in preparation for his restoration marked first in chapter seven and again in chapter eight by Thomas Mann's reiteration of the leitmotiv, "Sein Herz lebte" (*VIII*, 332; 336).

There remains the end of the story with its subtle mutation of the central leitmotiv. The heart is not mentioned in chapter nine, yet Tonio's letter to Lisaweta contains, with a plea that he will not be scolded, the confession of his love that belongs to the "Blonden und Blauäugigen, den hellen Lebendigen ..." Then as the Novelle closes, Tonio Kröger applies to this love what was said as the climax of chapter one about his living heart: "Sehnsucht ist darin und schwermütiger Neid und ein klein weig Verachtung und eine ganze keusche

Seligkeit" (*VIII*, 338). With this sentence the correlation of the first and second parts of *Tonio Kröger* is complete, revealing a symmetry of structure essentially equivalent to that of *Werther* and *Immensee*.

Though Thomas Mann's final transformation of the leitmotiv of the heart is clear indication of an intent in *Tonio Kröger* divergent from that of Goethe in *Werther*, the motif still points to the thematic bond between the two works.

—Lida Kirchberger, "Popularity as a Technique: Notes on "Tonio Kröger." *Monatshefte* 63, no. 4 (1971): pp. 323–24, 329–30.

T. J. REED ON THE CHOICE OF THE ARTIST

[T. J. Reed is a Fellow of the British Academy and Taylor Professor of German at Oxford University. He has written two books on Mann, *Death in Venice: Making and Unmaking a Master* and *Thomas Mann: The Uses of Tradition*, and has also edited a collection of Goethe's poems. In this excerpt he articulates the protagonist's difficult choice between the solitary life and the socially integrated one.]

The central theme of *Tonio Kröger* is usually said to be the opposition of 'Geist' and 'Leben'—that is of literary sensitivity and detachment on the one hand, and ordinary harmonious vitality on the other. Tonio Kröger certainly uses these ambitiously general terms himself in the conversation scene. But (as emerges from a careful reading of the story) it isn't simply a matter of Mind against Life, each element pitting itself without reservation against the other. For one thing, Life hardly seems to notice Mind—that is part of the trouble. And more importantly, Mind itself, as represented by Tonio Kröger, is inwardly divided, suffers from contradictory loyalties. The normality (as it seems to him) of socially integrated people, their naturalness and beauty—at least when they happen to be young and blonde and blue-eyed—are a reproach to what he does and always has instinctively done: to literary observation, analysis, and the recording of human behaviour. He suffers not just from being excluded from something he would like to have and enjoy, but from the fact that he accepts *it* is normal and *he* isn't. Far from being at daggers drawn with Life, he takes its side against himself, he suffers from an inferiority complex. It becomes the defining characteristic of 'Geist' as he embodies it that it tends to self-betrayal. Mann later describes this as 'irony'; but in practice it means that the status and value of literature and everything it stands for—reflection as against thoughtless action, breadth of human sympathy as against the uncritical will to power—is highly precarious.

Of course, the case for literature is put too. As a fated writer—and in various ways it is made clear that Tonio Kröger has only fulfilled a destiny that there were no two ways about—he knows what literature can do and has apparently given himself wholeheartedly to his profession:

> Er ergab sich ganz der Macht, die ihm als die erhabenste auf Erden erschien, zu deren Dienst er sich berufen fühlte, und die ihm Hoheit und Ehren versprach, der Macht des Geistes und Wortes, die lächelnd über dem unbewußten und stummen Leben thront. (*VIII*, 289–90)

No sign of an inferiority complex there, quite the reverse; and there are a number of contexts in which Mann and his characters express their irritation at that un-consciousness of Life, the 'unbewußter Typus' dominant in society, from the viewpoint of the superior knowledge and understanding that literature gives. Literature (as the passage just quoted goes on to say) penetrates the façade of pretentious phrases—'die großen Wörter'—reveals men's souls, and opens up the realities of the world that lie beneath the surface.

But all this is surveyed in narrative retrospect as an earlier stage of Tonio Kröger's outwardly successful career; and by the time he comes to talk his problems over with Lisaweta Iwanowna in the central conversation-piece, it is unease and the price of success that dominate. Literature comes to seem almost a Faustian pact, giving him knowledge but making him pay for it inexorably. Knowledge, 'Erkenntnis', both the process and the results it produces, now make him sick ('Erkenntnisekel'). Yet the literary consciousness is a thing which, once acquired, can't easily be got rid of or switched off. Tonio Kröger's situation parallels the biblical Fall of Man—which was also a matter of 'Erkenntnis'—and is thus, of course, part of a notorious German tradition going back to Kleist and Schiller. Tonio

Kröger is unable to return to the pre-conscious Garden of Eden, or a state of grace. He can only resolve (and this is the conclusion in his letter to Lisaweta that ends the novella) to moderate his critical consciousness with love, the bourgeois love for ordinary humanity which he compares to the Christian charity (in German, straightforwardly 'Liebe') of I Corinthians xiii.

—T. J. Reed, "Text and History: *Tonio Kröger* and the Politics of Four Decades." *Publications of the English Goethe Society* 57 (1986–87): pp. 40–42.

BEVERLEY DRIVER EDDY ON THE DEVELOPMENT OF THE PROTAGONIST

[Beverley Driver Eddy is Professor of German at Dickinson College. She wrote an introductory essay to a 1985 translation of *Dracula*, and is currently writing a biography of the Danish author Karin Michaelis. In the following extract she discusses the lesson gained by the protagonist in the book's final section.]

Because of their differing views, Tonio thinks of the literary author as a "charlatan" and a "criminal," while Lisaweta regards the author as a priest." Tonio, who now identifies with the wordy, immobilized Hamlet, can do nothing with Lisaweta's words of wisdom, even when she describes his condition as that of "a bourgeois who has taken the wrong turning, . . . a bourgeois manqué" (164). Yet he offers a remarkable confession, telling her, "You have a right to talk that way, . . . conferred upon you by your national literature, by the sublime writers of Russia; their work I will willingly worship as the sacred literature of which you speak" (159). Although he now regards literature as something that cripples people and hinders action, he admits that Russian literature does not do so. He acknowledges, in other words, that there are various kinds of literature that serve various purposes. (Mann's own interest in and use of Russian literature, especially his reading of Goncharov's *Oblomov* during his visit to Denmark, may form another area of investigation. See, e.g., Banuls, "Thomas Mann und die russische Literatur.")

Tonio had already tried using literature positively, as a bridge to intimacy and understanding. As a boy he tried in vain to persuade Hans to read Schiller's *Don Carlos*, thinking, "[T]hen they would have something in common, something they could talk about" (143). He soon learned, though, that the bourgeois citizens he longed to be with had no use for literature, that in fact literature was forbidden fruit for such carefree people. He had already said of Ingeborg, "Only people who do not read *Immensee* and never try to write anything like it can be as beautiful and lighthearted as you; that is the tragedy!" (148). Tonio now considers literature a curse that sets people apart from life. He proffers a litany of examples: the banker-novelist turned criminal, the actor who is nothing without his stage makeup, the lieutenant who becomes laughable when he writes poetry, and the papal castrati. Healthy people, he seems to say, don't need literature—it is something only for outcasts, outsiders, people who fall in the dance.

To resolve his inner conflicts, Tonio chooses not to go to Russia, in spite of his admission to Lisaweta that Russian literature has the power to heal and make one whole. Instead he seeks his remedy in Denmark, the land of Hamlet, his present figure of literary identification (see Heine; Marx; Matthias; Steffensen). (. . .)

The ultimate irony of the work is that, by experiencing the people in the Danish setting as literature, Tonio is able to objectify his own life and understand himself in ways he never had before. Tonio writes to his Russian friend to tell her that he now realizes how correct her analysis of him had been. He promises her that he will write better literature. By closing the letter to Lisaweta with the words he had used to end chapter 1, Mann suggests that *Tonio Kröger* is itself the realization of that promise (Swales, *A Study,* 33). At this point Mann and Tonio Kröger merge. This merging explains the striking passage in the second chapter, in which a mature Mann used a direct form of address to tell Ingeborg how much Tonio had loved her. It explains, too, the gentle irony and warm humor of the first chapters. It comes then as no surprise that the lesson Tonio learns in Denmark is one that Mann acknowledged in a 1924 Danish interview. When asked whether any Danish writer had a particular influence on his writing, he replied without hesitation: "Yes, Herman Bang.... I have read everything by him and learned a great deal from him" (Hansen and Heine, 67). In *Tonio Kröger* Mann suggests that what he had learned is humanity. For him, at least, *Litteratur* has the power to transform.

—Beverley Driver Eddy, "Teaching *Tonio Kröger* as Literature about Literature." *Approaches to Teaching Mann's Death in Venice and Other Short Fiction*, ed. Jeffrey B. Berlin (New York: The Modern Language Association of America, 1992): pp. 121–22, 125.

"Felix Krull"

Mann wrote "Felix Krull," an episodic account of a sophisticated criminal in the making, in 1911. Over 40 years later he developed it into a novel, *Confessions of Felix Krull, Confidence Man*, published just a year before his death. The story is typical of Mann's work in that it focuses on the dynamics between the audience and the artist, though in this instance the protagonist's art is his life. The conclusions made by Felix Krull are surprisingly illuminating, raising questions about art and its deceptive function.

In the opening paragraph, Felix explains that he has taken up his pen to make a record of his confessions. With his exceptionally large ego, however, Felix proves to be just as boastful as he is contrite. He expresses some initial doubt about his qualifications as a writer, but he also believes that his "instinct for good form," which has made him a successful criminal, will help compensate for his inexperience. He assures the reader that although he is a fraud by profession, the story he is about to tell is entirely true.

He begins with his origins, speaking fondly of his boyhood home in the Rhine valley. He particularly remembers family excursions in which his parents, his sister Olympia, and his godfather Maggotson were all present. He describes his father's company, a manufacturer of a now-extinct brand of wine. The company's product is a fitting emblem of the hapless Krulls: the bottle's elaborately designed label gives it an attractive exterior, but the contents it holds are substandard. Felix remembers how Engelbert, a failure with little confidence, was crushed by the insults he received from Maggotson about his terrible wine. Felix, however, unconditionally loved his father throughout childhood and forgives him his faults.

Next Felix describes his birth, which he claims was a slow delivery because he had no desire to enter the world. He explains that as a child he found a passion for sleeping that remained with him into adulthood. He rarely showed interest in socializing, often retreating into his private world of daydreams. He also frequently did impersonations, which never failed to impress his parents and Maggotson. Even when Felix grew older, and make-believe no longer interested his schoolmates, he continued with the activity, sometimes spending an entire day pretending to be a prince. During his solitary hours he would test the limits of his own will with odd exercises like making his pupils expand and contract on command.

Felix offhandedly mentions his father's affair with a governess. The scandal tainted the family's reputation, and as a result Felix's friends told him that they could no longer associate with him. But he was hardly upset by the news. He was more frustrated by his mother sending Engelbert to another town, where he could temporarily pursue a bachelor's life away from the public eye. Felix didn't like the decision because he felt his mother—in his mind guilty of a similar infidelity—had no right to pass judgment. It was easier to excuse his father's practices because "his follies were never without a certain ease and grace." Felix uses the same moral approach toward his own criminal pursuits.

Felix's next tells a story of a personal triumph when he was eight years old. After attending a string concert, he became inspired to mime one of the violinists. His parents found the imitation so charming that they arranged at the next concert to equip him with a violin and a vaselined bow and place him beside the conductor. Felix's charade impressed the audience so much that they showered him with praise afterwards. A Russian princess even took off her brooch and pinned it on Felix's chest as an award. He describes the day as one of the happiest of his life.

Felix then explains how he came to love role-playing over the course of modeling for Maggotson, an amateur painter. After Felix's godfather had him try on several costumes, he told him that he could convincingly portray any person, from any time period. The modeling sessions were so enjoyable that when Felix would have to return to his old self again, he became miserable. His early discomfort with his everyday existence sheds light on why he enjoys role-playing later as a fraud.

Perhaps the most revealing episode of Felix's confessions is his first experience at the theatre when he was 14 years old. During the play Felix, along with the rest of the audience, became transfixed by the star actor Müller-Rosé, onstage an individual of unparalleled beauty. Felix makes few observations about his performance, but goes into elaborate detail about the actor's looks and graceful style. After the performance Engelbert, a former acquaintance of Müller-

Rosé's, took Felix to meet him backstage, where the boy encountered the complete opposite of what he expected. "I shall never forget the disgusting sight that offered itself to my boyish eyes," Felix remembers. Müller-Rosé's face was covered with pimples and caked with thick makeup, and Felix marveled that the ugly person before him was the same individual that dazzled the audience earlier. The meeting illuminated for him the artist-audience dynamic, one in which the myth of the artist's perfection is formed. Felix takes advantage of his own audience's naiveté during his career as a con artist.

In his teenage years, Felix remembers having an increasing distaste for school. He eventually figured out how to avoid going by forging excuse letters. After the letters he tried more elaborate kinds of fraud, including faking illness. Although his shams were not entirely convincing, his parents—and even his doctor—responded with sympathy. They believed the lie that he was ill, Felix realized, for the same reason that the audience believed in Müller-Rosé's perfect beauty.

From his success at feigning illness Felix proceeds into the story of his early success as a thief. One day, upon stumbling on a fancy food store with no attendants at the counter, he stole a handful of candy and ran away. The situation presented itself several more times with the same success. Felix makes a concerted effort at this point to explain that his theft should not be considered a petty crime because *he* did it, a person with outstanding qualities, and not some common individual. He then recounts an affair he had with the older housemaid Genoveva. He insists that in staying true to his exemplary character, he never let his emotions get out of control during the relationship.

His meandering account finally reaches the tragic moment that forced him to leave his parents' house permanently. When Felix turned 18, the struggling wine business finally went bankrupt. He remembers feeling terrible for his father, who afterwards sank into a depression. With the closing of the family business, Felix learned that he had to leave school, after which he never received his graduation certificate. Engelbert made a few attempts to resurrect his enterprising career, but with little success. One day, five months after bankruptcy was declared, Olympia found Engelbert dead after having shot himself. While the rest of the family was in hysterics, Felix and Genoveva laid his father's body on a sofa. The story closes abruptly with the image of Felix weeping beside his dead father.

It is clear by the story's end why Felix wanted to escape his family circumstances and become a fraud. However, with the many points of similarity between him and his ill-fated relations, it is difficult for the reader to accept his claims of success. If his life of fraud was at all successful, it was only through the help of his gullible audience. Mann's story, and the novel into which it developed, engages his readers to examine their own role in helping create the mythos of the artist.

"Felix Krull"

Felix Krull is the self-admiring professional criminal whose written confessions comprise the story. He comes from a middle-class family beset with scandals; however, his imagination and passion for role-playing help divert him from feeling ashamed or isolated. He believes that because he is an exemplary individual, society should judge his deeds by a different moral standard than that of the common criminal.

Engelbert Krull is Felix's good-natured father and the manufacturer of an inferior champagne. A philanderer and a failure at business matters, he declares bankruptcy and a few months later commits suicide.

Olympia is Felix's older sister who finds little success as an actress. Felix believes she is licentious and has little respect for her.

Maggotson, Felix's godfather, is an amateur painter who retired early to live with the Krulls. After Felix models for his paintings, he convinces the boy of his exceptional talent for playing different roles in costume.

Müller-Rosé is the star actor whom Felix encounters during his first visit to the theatre. He is deceptively handsome onstage, and his charming impression on the audience reveals to Felix its naive faith in the actor's flawlessness.

Felix's mother is, in the words of her son, a woman of "insignificant mental parts." Felix criticizes her reaction to the affair between Engelbert and the governess, and condemns her flirting with a housepainter.

Genevova is the Krull's housemaid and becomes Felix's mistress when he is 16 years old. Unimpressed with the marriage proposals she has received from other men, she believes that her affair with Felix will help improve her social station.

Dr. Dusing is the opportunistic and incompetent doctor who diagnoses Felix when he feigns illness.

"Felix Krull"

Robert B. Heilman on the Author's Inspiration

[Robert B. Heilman, a former Professor Emeritus of English
at the University of Washington, retired from teaching in
1971, but is still a prolific writer. His critical works include
The Workings of Fiction and *The Southern Connection*, as
well as several introductions to Shakespeare's plays. Here
he considers Mann's inspiration in writing the story.]

Critics often allude to the elements of self-portraiture in Mann"s
works, and Mann himself speaks of an artistic work as "a realization
. . . of our individuality," even as "the sole and painful way we have
of getting the particular experience." (. . .)

[W]e must face the tantalizing question of Mann's motive in ren-
dering some phases of private history in picaresque, of the "secret
connections," as Mann himself puts it, that "I must lead from it [a
work of his] to earliest childhood dreams, if I am to consider myself
entitled to it, if I am to believe in the legitimacy of what I am doing."
For one thing, picaresque would be the least expectable mode of
autobiographic fiction; it would permit surprise, it would be new and
daring, it would be ironic and vastly playful—all ends that Mann
valued. It would disarm the audience, and, as an antidote to self-
love, it would be an extraordinary means of securing detachment, of
providing a wonderful distance and even freedom. The most convincing guess about Mann's leaving *Felix Krull* long unfinished
would rely on his remark that *The Magic Mountain* could not have
been written ten years earlier, since for the work he needed certain
experiences which had "to ripen within him." Surely this would be
true for *Felix Krull*, in which the severely limited view of man would
be possible to an artist of profound perceptions only when long
experience would make possible a curbing of his total vision, and of
which the comically disillusioned perspective, held serenely rather
than with querulous cynicism, is possible only to an artist of the
mature assurance conferred by long personal and professional

growth. Through such control he might give voice to self-criticism or guilt, perhaps effect a catharsis. If, as Hatfield says, "Werther and Aschenbach die in order that their creators may live," it may be that Felix had to live on in order that his creator might live with himself. Might not the disillusioned artist large enough to include himself in his own disillusionment say, "How like a rogue's life mine looks!" Within the capacious irony of the rogue's tale there lies, we may conjecture, humility: partly an oblique confession, partly an assumption of Everyman's rascality, a discovery of the heart masterfully transfigured into an urbane jest.

—Robert B. Heilman, "Variations on Picaresque (*Felix Krull*)." *Sewanee Review* 66, no. 4 (October–December 1958): pp. 560, 562–63.

ERICH HELLER ON THE ARTIST-CRIMINAL

[Erich Heller taught at Harvard, Yale, and the University of Chicago before becoming Avalon Emeritus Professor of the Humanities at Northwestern University. His works include *Thomas Mann: The Ironic German* and *The Disinherited Mind: Essays in Modern German Literature and Thought*. In this extract from *The Ironic German* he explains the comic dimension of Mann's "artist-criminal," a character type first encountered in *Tonio Kröger*.]

As early as *Tonio Kröger*, Thomas Mann was fascinated by the idea of the artist-criminal, the personified alliance between artistic creativeness and moral derangement. In that story the anecdote of the fraudulent banker who, while serving a prison sentence, becomes a writer, is the bizarre foil to the moral scruples of the young artist: "One might be rash enough to conclude," we read there, "that a man has to be at home in some kind of jail in order to become a poet." And again we saw how Tonio Kröger in a recess of his soul could not help agreeing with the police, the guardians of civic order, when mistakenly they contemplated his arrest. In Felix Krull this agreement expresses itself in comic abandon.

"Poetry came easily to me by virtue of the delicately balanced unreality of my existence." This is how this self-confessed impostor comments on his gift of lyrically exalted speech; and his creator, who has only just passed through the terrors of *Doctor Faustus*, knows that he shares this delicate fragility with a civilization hardly prepared any more to face the "seriousness of life." It is the unreality of the poetic existence, this most persistent and most personal of all the themes of Thomas Mann, that is at the same time humorously realized and outrageously parodied in *Felix Krull*. This book, therefore, is made of the stuff of which the world's great comic creations are made: a grave affliction of the soul resolved in laughter, a laughter which reverberates with many echoes of the writer's anxious passage through a melancholy age; and as the anxiety was not only his own, but the sadness of our civilization itself, Felix Krull stands a good chance of becoming a literary archetype. It is a measure of the seriousness of this jesting book that it might be given as its motto the words with which Keats expressed his poetic misery and which we previously quoted in connection with *Tonio Kröger*: "Not one word I ever utter can be taken for granted as an opinion growing out of my identical nature—how can it, when I have no nature?" Felix Krull too has no identical nature. He is the comic version of what Keats in the same letter (October 27, 1818) called "the chameleon Poet"—comic because his "creative imagination" expresses itself not in art but in life. But it would be wrong to say that he *plays* different parts. For roles can only be played by one who owns another identity; but Felix Krull *is* at every moment the imaginatively created person whose identity he has assumed.

> —Erich Heller, *Thomas Mann: The Ironic German*, (Cleveland, Ohio: The World Publishing Company, 1958): pp. 279–80.

MATTHEW GUREWITSCH ON MULTIPLE ROLES

[Matthew Gurewitsch is author of *When Stars Blow Out: A Fable of Fame in Our Time*, and has published reviews of books, theater, and music in *Harvard Magazine* and *The New Republic*. Here he demonstrates how the protagonist's malleable personality allows him to take on multiple roles.]

The major patterns of polarity in *Felix Krull* do not, of course, impinge on the reader's consciousness until he has made substantial headway into the narrative. Still, from the first, style hints at a habit of mind that delights in holding contrasting ideas poised in an elegant and precarious equilibrium. On the opening page of his memoirs, Felix Krull writes:

> mein Vater, wiewohl dick und fett, besass viel persönliche Grazie und legte stets Gewicht auf eine gewählte und durchsichtige Ausdrucksweise. (I.1, 5)

> [my father, though stout and fat, had much personal grace and always stressed the importance of expressing oneself fastidiously and transparently.]

It is at once apparent that—in matters of style at least—Felix is very much his father's son. But note the conjunction of "gewählt" and "durchsichtig": the two ideals here invoked are far from obviously harmonious. (. . .)

Felix's speech, full of lofty excursions and flashy vulgarity, refuses to stamp him either as an upstart or as a brahmin. Thus, on the level of language itself, we may observe how his nature partakes of many natures. He plays roles, but the roles cannot capture the full scope of his elusive spirit. Early in the novel, Felix describes his first visit to a theatre. On stage, Müller-Rosé, the star of the show, enchants his audience in the guise of a debonair dandy. But when Felix is brought backstage, he sees in the dressing room a creature he can only describe as "dies verschmierte und aussätzige Individuum" (I.5, 26), ["this smudged and leprous individual"]. Which is Müller-Rosé's "true" identity? Felix warns us not to presume to determine and makes the analogy of the performer to the glowworm: what is *its* true form? The unsightly bug or the bright flying ember? Well into the novel, he comments on his own dual existence as an elegant waiter and an elegant gentleman, saying:

> Verkleidet also war ich in jedem Fall, und die unmaskierte Wirklichkeit zwischen den beiden Erscheinungsformen, das Ichselber-Sein, war nicht bestimmbar, weil tatsächlich nicht vorhanden. (III.3, 179)

> [Either way I was in disguise, and the unmasked truth between the two appearances, the real me, was not determinable, for in fact it did not exist.]

Lorley extra cuvée, the acid brew from the cellars of Felix's father, Engelbert Krull, comes bottled in splendiferous glitter. Its packaging constitutes attempted fraud. The performer's case is not so clear-cut and is richly ambiguous. Felix Krull is himself a performer, and his world is a world of blurred contours. People, things, and events reach out to each other and intermesh. And this is already clearly prefigured in his verbal style.

> —M. Anatole Gurewitsch, "Counterpoint in Thomas Mann's *Felix Krull*." *Modern Fiction Studies* 22, no. 4 (Winter 1976–77): pp. 528, 529.

MICHAEL BEDDOW ON THE NARRATION

[Michael Beddow taught German at King's College London and Leeds University, and is author of *The Fiction of Humanity: Studies in the Bildungsroman from Wieland to Thomas Mann* and an analysis of *Doctor Faustus*. Here he analyzes how the narrator tells his story and exposes himself as a charlatan.]

Felix Krull is perhaps the most elusive of Thomas Mann's novels. One of the things that makes the work evade definitive description is the multitude of guises that the central figure assumes both as agent within the narrative and as narrator. Among the abundant secondary literature there are convincing and illuminating studies of Felix as a latter-day picaro; as a Bildungsroman hero *à rebours*; as an unwitting parodist of eighteenth-century confessional writing; as a comic embodiment of Mann's lifelong preoccupation with the problematic nature of artistic talent; and as a reincarnation of Hermes. (. . .)

To read *Felix Krull* competently is to become intensely aware that one is responding to a sophisticated piece of fiction. No attentive reader can complete the first page and still believe that he has before him either a real autobiography or the skilful imitation of one. An innocent reading has to give way to growing complicity in the fictive process by the third sentence at the very latest, where we encounter the claim, "... ich stamme aus feinbürgerlichem, wenn auch liederlichem, Hause" (265) ("... I stem from a high-class, if dissolute, family"). Like so much else in the finely-calculated language of this novel, the phrase defies adequate translation. To term one's origins 'feinbürgerlich' is to lay claim to an upper middle class background which is both refined and highly respectable; it also suggests that one is more anxious to pretend to such origins than confident of possessing them, since no genuine member of the social circles to which 'feinbürgerlich' refers would actually apply the word to himself. The last thing someone with pretensions to be 'feinbürgerlich' is likely to say about his origins is that they were 'liederlich', a word redolent of both slovenliness and dissipation. Yet this is what the narrating voice does say here. The insouciant collocation of "feinbürgerlich" and "liederlich" is the first of what proves to be a series of strategic incongruities in the text. The preceding two-and-a-half sentences have begun to initiate us into Felix's ideolect, which apparently displays the features normally characteristic of a semi-literate nonentity who is attempting to write in a 'cultivated' manner. The laboured patterning of a trivial message into an elaborate periodic structure, the use of pompous periphrases and limp epitheta ornantia are recognisably similar to the pretentiosities of popular memoir-writers at the turn of the century. We habitually associate this stylistic repertoire with a particular variety of reading-experience: stereotyped performances by the author generate and fulfil expectations of stereotypes in the reader, so that the text is read through a kind of self-sustaining interaction of literary received ideas. The writer as individual and the reader as individual remain inert, inactive: they are mere onlookers of a process in which individuality, 'originality', questioning of conventional notions are uncalled for. Hence the shock of "feinbürgerliche, wenn auch liederlichem", since it violates all stereotypes and reshapes our incipient conception of what kind of text is before us.

—Michael Beddow, "Fiction and Meaning in Thomas Mann's *Felix Krull.*" *Journal of European Studies* 10, no. 38 (June 1980): pp. 78–79.

MARTIN SWALES ON THE THEATER SCENE

[Martin Swales is Professor of German at University College London. He wrote *Thomas Mann: A Study* and *Studies of German Prose Fiction in the Age of European*

Realism. In this extract from his book on Mann, he illustrates the significance of the theater scene, in which the true identity of a star actor is revealed to the protagonist.]

One important scene concerns Felix's first visit to the theatre. A light-hearted operetta is being performed and the chief actor is one Müller-Rosé, a friend of Krull's father. He gives a masterly performance, bewitching in its skill, wit, and elegance. Felix and his father go backstage after the curtain has fallen, and a horrific scene greets their eyes. The dressing room is filthy, and Müller-Rosé himself is nothing short of hideous. The face behind the make-up is pale and puffy, the eyes watery and inflamed. But worst of all, the skin is covered in ugly, infected pimples and sores. The mask, it would seem, has fallen irrevocably—and with it, we assume, the scales from Felix's eyes. But nothing could be further from the case. For what Felix offers is a defence of the illusion which Müller-Rosé created on stage, an illusion which is the more precious and admirable for being, precisely, an illusion, a complete fabrication. And yet this illusion bewitched an audience full of ordinary, practical people. How could this be?

> Die erwachsenen und im üblichen Masse lebenskundigen Leute aber, die sich so willig, ja gierig von ihm betören liessen, mußten sie nicht wissen, daß sie betrogen wurden? Oder achteten sie in stillschweigendem Einverständnis den Betrug nicht für Betrug? Letzteres wäre möglich; denn genau überdacht: wann zeigt der Glühwurm sich in seiner wahren Gestalt,—wenn er als poetischer Funke durch die Sommernacht schwebt, oder wenn er als niedriges, unansehnliches Lebewesen sich auf unserm Handteller krümmt? Hüte dich, darüber zu entscheiden! (26)

> But these grown up people, who were to the usual extent versed in the ways of the world, allowed themselves so willingly—indeed avidly—to be led by the nose by him: surely they must have known that they were being deceived? Or was it the case that they, in tacit collusion, did not regard the deception as deception? That would be possible. For, if one thinks carefully about it—when does the glow worm show himself in his true shape? When he hovers as a poetic spark through the summer's night, or when he, as a lowly and unprepossessing creature, rolls himself into a ball in the palm of our hand? Be careful not to make the choice!

The audience has, quite simply, colluded with the fiction of Müller-Rosé's making. Perfectly sensible, serious people have let themselves be deluded—because illusions are important and life-enhancing. Krull does not spare the special pleading here: he addresses *his* audience, us the readers, directly and warns us against too simple an espousal of a kind of reality-and-authenticity principle. Indeed, he pushes his case further, for he suggests that in the audience's preparedness to collude with fictions (and, by implication, in our preparedness to do the same for Krull's narrative performance), we see human beings obeying one of the profoundest dictates of their nature:

> Hier herrscht augenscheinlich ein allgemeines, von Gott selbst der Menschennatur eingepflanztes Bedürfnis (. . .) hier besteht ohne Zweifel eine für den Haushalt des Lebens unentbehrliche Einrichtung. (26)

> Here we can see a general need at work, one implanted by God in human nature (. . .) here we have beyond doubt an agency which is an indispensable part of man's equipment for living.

We are concerned with something that is essential, with an inalienable human need: the need to make, and to subscribe to, fictions. Here we reach the heart of Krull's case. Fictions, like theatres, are luxuries: they would seem, then, to be 'optional extras', icing on the cake, as it were. But they are, so Krull argues, not optional (because they answer a primary need, 'Bedürfnis'); they are, quite simply, indispensable. To them we are all subject, Müller-Rosé's 'Parkettpublikum' no less than ourselves, the button-holed readers of Krull's memoirs.

—Martin Swales, *Thomas Mann: A Study*, (London: Heinemann, 1980): pp. 103–105.

RICHARD SPULER ON DECEPTION

[Richard Spuler is a Senior Lecturer in German and Slavic Studies at Rice University in Texas. He co-edited (with Theodore Gish) *Eagle in the New World: German*

Immigration to Texas and America. Here he draws an analogy between Felix Krull the rogue and Mann the writer,
each of whom feels the need to deceive his audience.]

Krull, in effect, is no Romantic artist playing God, creating a uni-
verse out of nothingness. His existence consists rather in a re-
arrangement of concrete matter (his own body!). In a sense he really "invents" nothing—he violates the matter before him, debases it.
He can also use the basest, most worthless material—as does
Müller-Rosé—as does Mann in telling Krull's story. When Krull
decides to act, as when he feigns sickness so as to remain home from
school, or his staged epileptic fit before the army doctor, he is convincing through a deception based on the contrived re-arrangement
of the given, and therefore a deception, "der den Namen des Betrugs
nicht durchaus verdient." The consequences of his success are two-
fold: on the one hand, the world of those whom he deceives appears
as an illusory one; on the other hand, his role as (con-) artist is
assigned a certain problematic ambivalence. While he harms no one,
his influence is problematic, owing as it is to life's own fascination
for "schöner Schein." In other words, the deception is—wanted.
Where Krull does go to great lengths to create form where substance
is mostly lacking, his purpose must be both rhetorical and aesthetic.
(. . .)

Krull characterizes his relationship to society and the world as
"widerspruchsvoll" (174). Simultaneously attracted to and yet dis-
tanced from this world, he literally lives a life of irony. Thus we find
his world always relativized, whether within the limited structure of
the sentences he writes "gesund, übrigens, wenn auch müde, sehr
müde" (5); within an episode (his attraction to the "form" of Müller-
Rosé and his repulsion when exposed to the corrupted "substance");
on a thematic level (the leitmotif of the *Doppelbild*); or within Krull
himself (the mythic, hermaphroditic figure). Precisely this precari-
ousness, which Krull calls "das zart Schwebende . . . meiner
Existenz" (279), offers him artistic freedom. He is the omniscient
observer and skilled narrator who delights in improving upon nature
itself (32). His "confessions" create the expectation on our part that
he will indulge in spontaneous self-revelation; instead, we get a
deliberate arrangement—not a serious "life," but an artistic effect.

As artist, he views his primary interest in affording pleasure rather than acting as social critic. He even admits to not being a critical observer: "Kritisch? Aber nein. Ich habe Sinn für die Formen und Charaktere des Lebens, der Natur, das ist alles" (234). His concern that the reader not fail to appreciate the artistry of his work as narrator stems from his preference for form and pleasure, not substance and criticism. The later Mann wrote that the artist was no "ursprünglich moralisclies Wesen, sondern ein ästhetisches," whose main occupation was "das Spiel . . . und nicht die Tugend." For Mann, ethics and aesthetics constitute a basic polarity. The fact that this "position" defines Krull in an hyperbolic degree resulting in parody) reveals the ambivalence at the very source of its creator.

> —Richard Spuler, "'Im Gleichnis leben zu dürfen': Notions of Freedom in Thomas Mann's *Felix Krull.*" *Archiv für das Studium der neueren Sprachen und Literaturen* 220 (1983): pp. 344, 345–46.

IRVIN STOCK ON THE PROTAGONIST'S TALENTS

[Irvin Stock, Professor Emeritus of English at University of Massachusetts–Boston, is author of *Ironic Out of Love: The Novels of Thomas Mann*. The following extract from that book concentrates on the gifts of the protagonist and how they help ingratiate him to the reader.]

Felix Krull (1954) might well seem an unlikely work of fiction to have been written by a philosophic novelist in his old age. The autobiography of a confidence man, and one who, in spite of a reference to time spent in prison, tells his life-story as if it were that of a lofty success destined to triumph by his gifts, the novel is a parody of the self-important, self-adoring artist—of Goethe in his autobiography, to begin with, but inevitably and deliberately of Thomas Mann as well. Moreover, it is the gayest, swiftest and funniest of his novels, and the most openly and happily sexual. True, the idea for the story came to Mann long before: he wrote Book I (about his hero's childhood) in 1911. True, too, that when he resumed the novel in 1951 (on the very page of manuscript where he had abandoned it), his view of its meaning had changed. Still, the old man went back to the story because it profoundly suited him. This is why he not only resumed the comically complacent tone, but also launched his hero on precisely the career that the earlier pages had promised. If reading the novel is for some of us like eating ice cream, this, I'm afraid, is a large part of the reason. It is the autobiography of a charmer whose driving motive is his desire for what we, as well as he, must call "the sweets of life," and whose distinctive gifts are precisely his exceptional potency in desiring and enjoying those sweets and his exceptional skill at winning them without slavery to a respectable job, by fraud and seduction. (. . .)

What draws that subject naturally into the open, and adds to the story a characteristic wealth of psychological, moral and philosophic reflection, is that this fraud is richly gifted with the awareness of self and others his profession requires. To him the idea that the artist is a con man presents itself in reverse as the proud conviction that the con man is an artist. As the mature man tells the story of his "early years," we are therefore getting, in effect, a conscious meditation—with examples—on the nature of the artist and his work, and getting it by way of that continuous parody-echo, now of Mann's great model Goethe, now of Mann himself.

From Goethe's autobiography come Krull's stately complacency of manner, his tendency to high-toned generalizations, and even a few virtual quotations. And from the Mann who made a point of the self-love that belonged to his talent, and who called his life "a happy, blessed life" because, in spite of troubles, "the foundation is, so to speak, sunny," and the artist, though "he deals with the absolute," is always entertaining himself and others with "a kind of child's play" (*Letters*, 373–376), comes Krull's bland references to his own physical beauty and to his parents. view of him as "a Sunday child" quite properly named Felix (happy). He echoes his author too when he calls his bad times merely "a cloud, as it were, through which the sun of my native luck continued to shine" (73). But of course, the real meat of the joke is in the way he delights all his life in "the glorious gift of imagination" which lifts him above the "dull and limited" others (8).

Not only does our hero play from childhood on the "game" of pretending to be what he is not—the frowning Kaiser, a violin prodigy (brilliantly manipulating his bow on greased and soundless strings), the officer, bullfighter and other types he models for his artist godfather, looking each one "to the life." When his "child's play" grows serious, it succeeds, he tells us, because it always has "a higher truth at its root" (31). Thus he gets out of a day of school by convincing not only his mother but a doctor that he is sick, and he can do so, he tells us, because, being "of finer stuff," he is on familiar terms with suffering and can create a "compelling and effective reality out of sheer inward knowledge . . . and the daring exploitation of my own body" (34). In short, Krull deceives as the novelist does, by expressing what is true to the human nature he shares with us all, if not to his particular self of the moment.

—Irvin Stock, *Ironic Out of Love: The Novels of Thomas Mann*, (Jefferson, N.C.: McFarland, 1994): pp. 202, 204–205.

Thomas Mann

Little Herr Friedemann. 1898.

Buddenbrooks. 1901.

Tonio Kröger. 1903.

Tristan. 1903.

Fiorenza. 1905.

Bilse und ich. 1906.

Royal Highness. 1909.

Death in Venice. 1912.

Reflections of a Non-Political Man. 1918.

A Man and His Dog. 1919.

The Magic Mountain. 1924.

Account of My Stay in Paris. 1926.

Mario and the Magician. 1930.

Sketch of My Life. 1930.

The Sufferings and Greatness of the Masters. 1933.

The Tales of Jacob. 1933.

The Young Joseph. 1934.

The Suffering and Greatness of the Masters. 1935.

The Stories of Three Decades. 1936.

Joseph in Egypt. 1939.

The Beloved Returns: Lotte in Weimar. 1939.

The Transposed Heads. 1940.

Joseph the Provider. 1943.

Doctor Faustus. 1947.

The Story of a Novel. 1949.

The Holy Sinner. 1951.

The Black Swan. 1953.

Confessions of Felix Krull, Confidence Man. 1954.

Essays on Schiller. 1955.

Death in Venice and Seven Other Stories. 1989.

Thomas Mann

Amory, Frederic. "The Classical Style of 'Der Tod in Vendedig.'" *Modern Language Review* 59 (1964): 399–409.

Apter, T. E. *Thomas Mann: The Devil's Advocate.* New York: New York University Press, 1979.

Barnouw, Dagmar. "Fascism, Modernity, and the Doctrine of Art from *Mario and the Magician* to *Doctor Faustus.*" *Michigan Germanic Studies* 28 (Spring 1992): 48–64.

Baron, Frank. "Sensuality and Morality in Thomas Mann's 'Tod in Venedig.'" *Germanic Review* 45 (1970): 115–25.

Beddow, Michael. "Fiction and Meaning in Thomas Mann's *Felix Krull.*" *Journal of European Studies* 10 (June 1980): 77–92.

Bloom, Harold, ed. *Thomas Mann.* New York: Chelsea House Publishers, 1986.

Bolkosky, Sidney. "Thomas Mann's 'Disorder and Early Sorrow': The Writer as Social Critic." *Contemporary Literature* 22 (Spring 1981): 218–33.

Braverman, Albert, and Larry Nachman. "The Dialectic of Decadence: An Analysis of Thomas Mann's 'Death in Venice.'" *Germanic Review* 45 (1970): 289–98.

Court, Franklin E. "Deception and the 'Parody of Externals' in Thomas Mann's 'Disorder and Early Sorrow.'" *Studies in Short Fiction* 12 (Spring 1975): 186–89.

Dyson, A. E. "The Stranger God: 'Death in Venice.'" *Critical Quarterly* 13 (1971): 5–20.

Eddy, Beverley Driver. "Teaching *Tonio Kröger* as Literature about Literature." *Approaches to Teaching Mann's* Death in Venice *and Other Short Fiction*, ed. Jeffrey B. Berlin. New York: The Modern Language Association of America, 1992.

Eggenschwiller, David. "The Very Glance of Art: Ironic Narrative in Thomas Mann's Novellen." *Modern Language Quarterly* 48 (1987): 59–85.

Ezergailis, Inta M., ed. *Critical Essays on Thomas Mann*. Boston: G. K. Hall, 1988.

Farrelly, D. J. "Apollo and Dionysus Interpreted in Thomas Mann's 'Der Tod in Venedig.'" *New German Studies* 3 (1975): 1–15.

Feuerlicht, Ignace. *Thomas Mann*. Boston: Twayne Publishers, 1968.

Geulen, Eva. "Resistance and Representation: A Case Study of Thomas Mann's "Mario and the Magician." *New German Critique* 23 (Spring–Summer 1996): 3–30.

Glebe, William V. "The Artist's 'Disease' in Some of Thomas Mann's Earliest Tales." *Books Abroad* 39 (1965): 261–68.

Good, Graham. "The Death of Language in 'Death in Venice.'" *Mosaic* 5 (1971): 43–52.

Grautoff, Otto. "Thomas Mann: The Stylist of Suffering." *Die Gegenwart* 64 (1903): 102–103. Reprinted in *Thomas Mann*, ed. Michael Minden. London: Longman, 1995.

Gronicka, André von. *Thomas Mann: Profile and Perspectives*. New York: Random House, 1970.

Gurewitsch, M. Anatole. "Counterpoint in Thomas Mann's *Felix Krull*." *Modern Fiction Studies* 22 (Winter 1976–77): 525–42.

Hatfield, Henry. "Mario and the Magician." In *The Stature of Thomas Mann*. New York: New Directions, 1947.

———, ed. *Thomas Mann: A Collection of Critical Essays*. Englewood Cliffs, N.J.: Prentice-Hall, 1964.

Hayman, Ronald. *Thomas Mann: A Biography*. New York: Scribner, 1995.

Heilbut, Anthony. *Thomas Mann: Eros and Literature*. New York: Knopf, 1996.

Heilman, Robert B. "Variations on Picaresque (*Felix Krull*)." *Sewanee Review* 66 (October–December 1958): 547–77.

Heller, Erich. "Parody, Tragic and Comic: Mann's *Doctor Faustus* and *Felix Krull*." *Sewanee Review* 66 (1958): 519–46.

———. *Thomas Mann: The Ironic German*. Cleveland, Ohio: The World Publishing Company, 1958.

Hollingdale, R. J. *Thomas Mann: A Critical Study*. Lewisburg, Pa.: Bucknell University Press, 1971.

Jonas, Ilsedore. *Thomas Mann and Italy,* trans. Betty Crouse. University: The University of Alabama Press, 1979.

Kirchberger, Lida. "Popularity as a Technique: Notes on 'Tonio Kröger.'" *Monatshefte* 63 (Winter 1971): 321–34.

Kraft, Quentin G. "Life Against 'Death in Venice.'" *Criticism* 7 (1965): 217–23.

Leppmann, Wolfgang. "Time and Place in 'Death in Venice.'" *German Quarterly* 48 (1975): 66–75.

Lesér, Esther H. *Thomas Mann's Short Fiction: An Intellectual Biography*, ed. Mitzi Brunsdale. Rutherford, N.J.: Fairleigh Dickinson University Press, 1989.

Lukács, Georg. *Essays on Thomas Mann*, trans. Stanley Mitchell. New York: Grosset & Dunlap, 1964.

Mandel, Siegfried. "Mann's *Mario and the Magician*, Or Who Is Silvestra?" *Modern Fiction Studies* 25 (Winter 1979–80): 593–612.

Martin, John S. "Circean Seduction in Three Works by Thomas Mann." *Modern Language Notes* 78 (1963): 346–52.

McClain, William H. "Wagnerian Overtones in 'Der Tod in Venedig.'" *Modern Language Notes* 79 (1964): 481–95.

McIntyre, Allan J. "Determinism in *Mario and the Magician*." *Germanic Review* 52 (May 1977): 205–16.

McWilliams, J. R. "The Failure of a Repression: Thomas Mann's 'Tod in Venedig.'" *German Life & Letters* 20 (1966–67): 233–41.

Nelson, Donald F. *Portrait of the Artist as Hermes*. Chapel Hill: The University of North Carolina Press, 1971.

Nicholls, R. A. "Death in Venice." In *Nietzsche in the Early Work of Thomas Mann*, ed. A. H. Rowbotham. Berkeley: University of California Press, 1955.

Northcote-Bade, James. "The Background to the 'Liebestod' Plot Pattern in the Works of Thomas Mann." *The Germanic Review* 59 (1984): 11–18.

————. "Der Tod in Venedig' and 'Felix Krull': The Effect of the Interruption in the Composition of Thomas Mann's 'Felix Krull' Caused by 'Der Tod in Venedig.'" *Deutsche Vierteljahrsschrift für Literaturwissenschaft und Geistesgeschichte (DVLG)* 52 (1978): 271–78.

O'Neill, Patrick. "Dance and Counterdance: A Note on 'Tonio Kröger.'" *German Life & Letters* 29 (1975–76): 291–95.

Parkes, Ford B. "The Image of the Tiger in Thomas Mann's 'Tod in Venedig.'" *Studies in Twentieth Century Literature* (1978): 73–83.

Pike, Burton. "Thomas Mann and the Problematic Self." *Publications of the English Goethe Society* 37 (1967): 120–41.

Reed, T. J. "Text and History: *Tonio Kröger* and the Politics of Four Decades." *Publications of the English Goethe Society* 57 (1986–87): 39–54.

————. *Death in Venice: Making and Unmaking a Master.* New York: Twayne Publishers, 1994.

————. *Thomas Mann: The Uses of Tradition.* Oxford: Clarendon Press, 1996.

Rey, William. "Tragic Aspects of the Artist in Thomas Mann's Work." *Modern Language Quarterly* 19 (1958): 195–203.

Ritter, Naomi, ed. *Death in Venice.* Boston: Bedford Books, 1998.

Robertson, Ritchie, ed. *The Cambridge Companion to Thomas Mann.* New York: Cambridge University Press, 2002.

Rockwood, Heidi M., and Robert J. R. Rockwood. "The Psychological Reality of Myth in 'Der Tod in Venedig.'" *Germanic Review* 59 (1984): 137–41.

Rotkin, Charlotte. "Oceanic Animals: Allegory in 'Death in Venice.'" *Papers on Language & Literature* 23 (Winter 1987): 84–88.

Slochower, Harry. "Thomas Mann's 'Death in Venice.'" *American Imago* 26 (1969): 99–122.

Spuler, Richard. "'Im Gleichnis leben zu dürfen': Notions of Freedom in Thomas Mann's *Felix Krull.*" *Archiv für das Studium der neueren Sprachen und Literaturen* 220 (1983): 343–50.

Stewart, Walter K. "'Der Tod in Venedig': The Path to Insight." *Germanic Review* 53 (1978): 50–55.

Stock, Irvin. *Ironic Out of Love: The Novels of Thomas Mann.* Jefferson, N.C.: McFarland, 1994.

Swales, Martin. *Thomas Mann: A Study.* London: Heinemann, 1980.

Symington, Rodney. "Tonio Kröger's Conversation with Lisaweta Iwanowna: Difficulties and Solutions." *Approaches to Teaching Mann's* Death in Venice *and Other Short Fiction,* ed. Jeffrey B. Berlin. New York: The Modern Language Association of America, 1992.

Tarbox, Raymond. "'Death in Venice': The Aesthetic Object as Dream Guide." *American Imago* 26 (1969): 123–44.

Tobin, Robert. "Why Is Tadzio a Boy?: Perspectives on Homoeroticism in *Death in Venice.*" *Thomas Mann: Death in Venice,* ed. Clayton Koelb. New York: W. W. Norton & Company, 1994.

Traschen, Isadore. "The Uses of Myth in 'Death in Venice.'" *Modern Fiction Studies* 11 (Summer 1965): 165–79.

Travers, Martin. "The Call to Unreason: *Mario and the Magician.*" In *Thomas Mann.* New York: St. Martin's Press, 1992.

Turner, David. "Balancing the Account: Thomas Mann's *Unordnung und frühes Leid.*" *German Life and Letters* 12 (January 1999): 43–57.

White, Richard. "Love, Beauty, and Death in Venice." *Philosophy and Literature* 14 (April 1990): 53–64.

Wilkinson, Elizabeth M. Introduction to *Tonio Kröger.* Oxford: Basil Blackwell, 1944.

Wilson, Kenneth G. "The Dance as Symbol and Leitmotiv in Thomas Mann's *Tonio Kröger.*" *Germanic Review* 29 (December 1954): 282–87.

Woodward, Anthony. "The Figure of the Artist in Thomas Mann's 'Tonio Kroger' and 'Death in Venice.'" *English Studies in Africa* 9 (1966): 158–67.

ACKNOWLEDGEMENTS

"Wagnerian Overtones in 'Der Tod in Venedig'" by William H. McClain from *Modern Language Notes* 79 © 1964 by Johns Hopkins University Press. Reprinted by Permission.

"The Uses of Myth in 'Death in Venice'" by Isadore Traschen from *Modern Fiction Studies* XI:2 (1965), 165-166. © Purdue Research Foundation. Reprinted by permission of the Johns Hopkins University Press.

"Failure of a Repression: Thomas Mann's 'Tod in Venedig'" by J.R. McWilliams from *German Life & Letters,* Vol. XX © 1967 by Blackwell Publishers. Reprinted by Permission.

Jonas, B. Ilsedore. *Thomas Mann and Italy* © 1979 by the University of Alabama Press. Reprinted by permission of Carl Winter Universitatsverlag.

"Oceanic Animals: Allegory in 'Death in Venice'" by Charlotte Rotkin from *Papers on Language & Literature* 23, no. 1 © 1987 by Southern Illinois University. Reprinted by Permission.

White, Richard. "Love, Beauty and Death in Venice." *Philosophy and Literature* 14:1 (1990), 56-58. © The Johns Hopkins University Press. Reprinted by permission of the Johns Hopkins University Press.

"Why Is Tadzio a Boy?: Perspectives on Homoeroticism in *Death in Venice*" by Robert Tobin from *Thomas Mann: Death in Venice* © 1994 by W.W. Norton. Reprinted by Permission.

"Mario and the Magician" by Henry C. Hatfield from *The Stature of Thomas Mann* © 1947 by New Directions Books. Reprinted by Permission.

"Determinism in *Mario and the Magician*" by Allan J. McIntyre from *Germanic Review* 52, no. 3 © 1977 by Columbia University Press. Reprinted by Permission.

T.E. Apter. *Thomas Mann: The Devil's Advocate* © 1979 by New York University Press. Reproduced with permission of Palgrave Macmillan.

"The Dance as Symbol and Leitmotiv in Thomas Mann's *Tonio Kröger*" by Kenneth G. Wilson from *The Germanic Review* 29, no. 4 © 1954 by Columbia University Press. Reprinted by Permission.

Kirchberger, Lida. "Popularity as a Technique: Notes on 'Tonio Kröger'". *Monatshefte*, Vol. 63, No. 4. © 1971. Reprinted by permission of the University of Wisconsin Press.

"Text and History: 'Tonio Kröger' and the Politics of Four Decades" by T.J. Reed from *The English Goethe Society,* Vol. 57 © 1988 by the English Goethe Society. Reprinted by Permission.

"Teaching 'Tonio Kröger' as Literature about Literature" by Beverley Driver Eddy from *Approaches to Teaching Mann's 'Death in Venice' and Other Short Fiction* © 1992 by The Modern Language Association of America. Reprinted by Permission.

"Variations on Picaresque (*Felix Krull*)" by Robert B. Heilman. First published in the Sewanee Review, vol. 66, no. 4, Fall 1958. © 1958 by the University of the South. Reprinted with the permission of the editor.

Heller, Erich. *Thomas Mann: The Ironic German* © 1958 by The World Publishing Company. Reprinted by Permission.

Gurewitsch, M. Anatole. "Counterpoint in Thomas Mann's 'Felix Krull'" from Modern Fiction Studies 22:4 (1976-1977), 528-529. © Purdue Research Foundation. Reprinted by permission of the Johns Hopkins University Press.

"Fiction and Meaning in Thomas Mann's 'Felix Krull'" by Michael Beddow from *Journal of European Studies* Vol. 10, Part 2, no. 38 © 1980 by Alpha Academic. Reprinted by Permission.

Swales, Martin. *Thomas Mann: A Study* © 1980 by Heinemann. Reprinted by Permission.

"'Im Gleichnis leben zu dürfen': Notions of Freedom in Thomas Mann's 'Felix Krull'" by Richard Spuler © 1983 from *Archiv für das Studium der neueren Sprachen und Literaturen* 220 by Erich Schmidt Verlag GmbH & Co. Reprinted by Permission.

Ironic Out of Love: The Novels of Thomas Mann by Irvin Stock © 1994 by McFarland & Company, Inc. Reprinted by Permission.

Themes and Ideas

multiple roles played by Krull in, 96–98; narration in, 98–99; plot summary of, 89–92; theater scene in, 99–101

JOSEPH AND HIS BROTHERS, 11

MAGIC MOUNTAIN, 11, 13, 67

MANN, THOMAS: Abel Cornelius character and, 65–66; on the artist-criminal, 95; biography of, 12–14; literary influences on, 87–88; literary works by, 11, 106; on mythical/psychological thought, 47–48; works about, 107–11; World War II and, 13

MARIO AND THE MAGICIAN, 9, 11, 36–53; Signora Angiolieri in, 38; art and politics connection in, 48–49, 50; atmospheric setting in, 45; audience in, 45–46; brass youth in, 37, 38; Cavaliere Cipolla in, 37–38, 41–42, 44, 45–46, 47, 51; characters in, 40; critical views on, 41–53; determinism in, 43–44, 49–50; fascism and, 36, 38, 41–43, 49, 51–53; German family in, 36-37, 45, 46; Mario in, 37, 38, 46, 52; narrator in, 36, 38, 46, 51–52, 53; Nazi Germany and, 50–51; plot summary of, 36–39; power dynamics in, 44–46; Roman gentleman in, 38; themes in, 51

TONIO KROGER, 9–10, 11, 72–88; autobiographical elements in, 12, 87–88; awareness and alienation of artist in, 77–78; bourgeois life in, 81–82; characters in, 76; critical views on, 77–88; Hans Hansen in, 72, 74, 77–78, 81–82; Inge Holm in, 72–73, 74, 81–82; Lisabeta Ivaanovna in, 73, 78, 81, 86; Francois Knaak in, 72; Consuelo Kröger in, 72, 80; Consul Kröger in, 72, 80; lesson learned by Tonio in, 87–88; Officer Peterson in, 74; plot summary of, 72–75; solitary vs. socially integrated life in, 84–86; sources of inspiration for, 82–84; symbolism of dance in, 79–81; Tonio's opinion on literature in, 86–87; Magdalena Vermehren in, 72;